DOOR TO DOOR

A GUIDE TO TRANSPORT FOR PEOPLE WITH DISABILITIES

London: HMSO

Applications for reproduction should be made to HMSO
First published 1982
Fourth Edition 1992.

ISBN 0 11 551116 4

PREFACE

This is the fourth edition of Door to Door. Since it was first published in 1982, there have been many developments in the range of transport available to and accessible by people with disabilities; from accessible public transport to personal mobility and specialised services. But information about those services is still too often lacking, and without information the opportunity to travel, or indeed for day-to-day independent mobility, is very limited.

The purpose of Door to Door is to bring together basic information about transport for people with mobility problems. If you have been disabled for some time, the guide is a useful source of reference and may perhaps put you in touch with some new opportunities. If you are recently disabled, you may find the guide a starting point from which to explore the range of mobility and transport opportunities open to you.

The guide covers all forms of transport both for local and longer distance journeys and is intended to give you contact points for further information. The guide cannot tell you what transport services you will find specifically in your area but it does give a list of contacts in your County or Region who will be able to help you further.

This fourth edition of Door to Door has been produced for the Department of Transport's Disability Unit by TRIPSCOPE, the nationwide travel and transport information and advice service for disabled and elderly people. TRIPSCOPE offers free help with information about any travel problem which a disabled or elderly person may have and with detailed journey planning. Further and more detailed information about any of the schemes and facilities listed in this guide is available from TRIPSCOPE (more details about TRIPSCOPE are given in Chapter 2, "Planning Your Journey").

Whilst every care has been taken to ensure that the information given is accurate at the time of going to press (June 1992), changes are bound to occur after the Guide is in circulation. If you are aware of important changes that should be made in the next edition, please write to the Disability Unit at the Department of Transport (the address is given in Chapter 1).

DISABILITY UNIT
DEPARTMENT OF TRANSPORT

CONTENTS

INTRODUCTION v

How to use this guide

1. GETTING STARTED 1

This chapter gives an outline of the main benefits and allowances available and where to get more information about them. It also explains how to obtain the equipment you may need, from walking aids to wheelchairs.

2. PLANNING YOUR JOURNEY 11

This briefly reviews the main organisations concerned with transport for people with disabilities.

3. LOCAL TRIPS 17

Most people are mainly concerned about making local trips. This chapter suggests what you should take into account when deciding how to make the trip. There is information about travel by public transport; bus, metro or underground, and local rail services. It also covers taxis, an increasing number of which are fully accessible, and the growing range of transport services provided by voluntary organisations. There is a section on transport for particular purposes: shopping, work, day centres, hospital and school or college.

4. TRAVELLING IN AND ACROSS LONDON 39

Because so many journeys start or finish in London, or involve crossing London, this chapter deals with special facilities and services available, whether public, private or voluntary. There is a separate section on transport especially for visitors to London and one on transport especially for London residents. For those who have to cross London as part of a longer journey there is a section on "Getting Across London".

5. TRAVELLING FURTHER AFIELD 53

There are often different problems involved in travelling longer distances, to unfamiliar places. This chapter explains how to get the help you need when travelling further afield in Britain by rail, coach, air and ferry, as well as what door-to-door services can help.

CONTENTS

INTRODUCTION
HOW TO USE THIS GUIDE

This Guide is designed to help you find all the information you need in connection with transport for people with disabilities. Our aim has been to make it as useful to organisations which give advice and information as to you if you have a disability. Whether you have a severe mobility handicap, or just have a bit of trouble getting out and about, the Guide provides essential information on how to make sure you get all the help you need in planning and making your journey.

In the following chapters you will find information on a wide range of transport topics, together with the organisations to contact for more details. In a guide this size we can only give a summary of the key points about transport services and facilities for people with special needs, but we do list the organisations which can help you with more detailed, local information.

In each chapter you will find:

- general information about the particular subject

- references to useful books and leaflets

- concessions which may be applicable

- summaries or lists of key information or contacts highlighted in special panels

- a list of the names, addresses and telephone numbers of all the organisations mentioned.

The Guide begins with a chapter on state benefits and allowances to which you may be entitled and information about wheelchairs and other equipment to help you in "Getting Started". Chapter 2 follows with some general information on "Planning Your Journey", and subsequent chapters are concerned with different sorts of journey: local, long-distance, going abroad, going on holiday. There is a separate chapter on "Cars and Driving" and a special chapter on "Travelling In and Across London". London gets a special mention because so many journeys start or finish in London, or involve getting across the capital.

Throughout this Guide the expression "(w) accessible" is used to indicate that a transport service or facility is fully wheelchair accessible.

The three Appendices at the back of the Guide contain:

- a list of the books and guides mentioned; and

- a geographical directory which lists separately for England, Scotland and Wales:

  – the major national disability and voluntary organisations

  – organisations in each County or Region which can give more detailed information

  (There is not enough space to list *local* disability or voluntary organisations but they can usually be found through the national offices listed or the appropriate 'umbrella' organisation given in each county/region.)

- a subject index of all the topics covered by this guide

1. GETTING STARTED

▶ BENEFITS AND ALLOWANCES

Checking whether you are receiving the benefits and allowances to which you are entitled is a good starting point. There is a wide range of benefits and allowances intended to help people with disabilities but it can be difficult, and sometimes confusing, trying to find out what you are entitled to claim.

Useful Publications

The Departments of Health (DH) and Social Security (DSS) produce several leaflets on benefits which you may find useful. They include:

"Which Benefit?" (DSS Leaflet FB2). A guide to the Social Security and the National Health Service benefits you can claim.

"Sick or Disabled?" (DSS leaflet FB28). A guide to the benefits if you are sick or disabled for a few days or more.

"Social Security" (DSS leaflet HB5). A guide to non-contributory benefits for disabled people.

"Equipment and Services for people with disabilities", (DH leaflet HB6).

These leaflets are available free of charge from:

- local Social Security offices (you can find the address in the phone book under 'Social Security' or 'Health and Social Security');

or by post from:

- DH and DSS Leaflets Unit;

- Welsh Office (WO) Local Authority Social Services Division (LASSIB).

Some leaflets are also available from post offices.

You can also get details of benefits and allowances from the latest editions of the following publications which are regularly updated:

"Disability Rights Handbook", available from the Disability Alliance;

"Directory for Disabled People", available from the Royal Association for Disability and Rehabilitation (RADAR) and bookshops.

Where to get Helpful Advice and Information

If you are in doubt about what you are *entitled* to claim – and not just about transport matters – there are several organisations which will be happy to help. You can contact:

- any local DSS office (England and Wales) or local SHHD office (Scotland);

- the DSS freeline telephone service (0800–666555) which will give general advice and information on all Social Security benefits (there is no charge for the phone call or the information);

- the Disablement Income Group (DIG);

- local branches of: Citizens Advice Bureau;
              Disablement Information Advice Line (DIAL);

- local associations of and for disabled people.

Entitlement to some benefits or local concessions may depend on being registered with your local authority as a disabled person. You can get information on registration procedures and on the full range of local services and concessions for people with disabilities from your local authority Social Services Department (Social Work Department in Scotland).

If you are – or hope to be – in work, you may also need to be included on the separate Disabled Persons' Employment Register. Ask for details at your local Jobcentre.

Disability Living Allowance (DLA)

> **On 6 April 1992 Disability Living Allowance (DLA) replaced Attendance Allowance for people disabled before the age of 65, and Mobility Allowance.**

DLA brings together the old Mobility Allowance and the old Attendance Allowance into one new allowance. It is a tax-free benefit for people who have a care or mobility need which arises from a disability or illness before the age of 65. It is not income related.

The amount of benefit paid depends on the need for help with getting around – this is called the 'Mobility Component'; and on how much care is required – this is called the 'Care Component'. The Mobility Component is paid at one of two rates. The Care Component is paid at one of three rates.

Attendance Allowance remains for people disabled after the age of 65.

IF YOU RECEIVED MOBILITY ALLOWANCE (or Attendance Allowance) you will have been transferred automatically to DLA from April 1992. The Mobility Allowance upper age limit of 80 years has been removed, and providing you continue to satisfy the other conditions you will continue to receive the benefit indefinitely.

IF YOU DID NOT RECEIVE MOBILITY ALLOWANCE you may be able to get the DLA (Mobility Component) if you meet the conditions summarised below. Claims will only be accepted for people aged 5 years or over and who apply before their 66th birthday.

The higher rate applies if the person

- is unable or virtually unable to walk; or

- has had both legs amputated at or above the ankle; or

- was born without legs or feet; or

- is both deaf and blind; or

- is severely mentally impaired and displays severe behavioural problems.

The lower rate applies when the person can walk but needs supervision out of doors.

One or other of those conditions has to have existed for three months and be likely to continue for at least a further six months.

An explanatory leaflet on DLA and on how to claim is available from local DSS offices, most public libraries and post offices, or from the DSS Leaflet Unit.

War Pensioners' Mobility Supplement

If you are a War Pensioner and you have a serious walking problem which has been caused by the disablement for which you receive the War Pension, you may be able to claim War Pensioners' Mobility Supplement.

The supplement cannot be paid at the same time as the DLA (Mobility Component), or while a vehicle is on loan to you under the War Pensioners' Vehicle Scheme. However, if you have a car under this scheme you can surrender it and switch to the Mobility Supplement at any time.

For further information you should see leaflet:

● MPL 153 "Guide For the War Disabled", or

● FB 16 "Sick Or Injured Through Service In the Armed Forces".

They are available from local DSS offices or the DSS Leaflets Unit, or you can write direct to the DSS War Pensioners' Mobility Supplement Section.

Invalid Three-wheelers (Trikes)

If you have an invalid three-wheeler, you can switch to the higher rate of DLA (Mobility Component) instead, even if you are over the age of 65.

For full details you should contact:

(in England)   DSS N9C Invalid Vehicle Service;

(in Scotland)   SHHD;

(in Wales)   Artificial Limb and Appliance Centre, Cardiff.

▶ EQUIPMENT

Walking Aids and Appliances

Crutches, walking sticks, walking frames and similar aids are supplied free of charge by the National Health Service (NHS). Your doctor will refer you to the hospital physiotherapy or occupational therapy department who will decide what walking aid will help you most. They will also train you to use it. Sometimes your local authority's Social Services Department (Social Work Department in Scotland) can supply walking aids through its own occupational therapy service.

You can find out more from the following leaflets:

● "Help With Mobility: Getting Around". DSS leaflet HB4 available from DSS local offices (SHHD in Scotland);

● "Walking Aids: List 9". Available from the Disabled Living Foundation (DLF);

● "Walking Equipment: List 13". Available from Disability Scotland.

Wheelchairs

Choosing a Wheelchair

There are various types of wheelchair available, either to buy or to obtain on permanent or short term loan. Before you get one, think carefully about what you need it for and the places where you want to use it. They vary from manually propelled to powered wheelchairs and scooters, some with a top speed of 8 mph, which can also be used on the road. Most outdoor wheelchairs fold up and can be taken in a car.

Whatever you choose, it is important that the wheelchair fits you properly, even if you don't intend to use it all the time. There are 35 Disabled Living Centres (DLCs) throughout the country, which can give advice and information on wheelchairs as well as a wide variety of other equipment. They can demonstrate the equipment which can be seen there on permanent exhibition, so you can make a well-informed decision before choosing the equipment which best suits your needs. You can find out where your nearest DLC is situated by contacting the Disabled Living Centres Council. A useful leaflet on wheelchairs is produced by the DLF – "Wheelchairs: List 10".

NHS Wheelchairs on Permanent Loan

If you have a permanent mobility problem you can obtain a wheelchair on permanent loan from the National Health Service (NHS). Since April 1991 the NHS wheelchair service has generally been provided by District Health Authorities (DHA). To obtain an NHS wheelchair you will need to be referred to the DHA by your doctor.

The following information generally applies to NHS loans, but do check with your DHA or nearest DLC to find out what arrangements apply in your particular case.

Three main types of wheelchair are provided:

- traditional manual wheelchairs (push or self-propelling);
- powered wheelchairs (indoor use only);
- powered wheelchairs (short-distance outdoor use/attendant controlled).

They are provided free of charge and on permanent loan if you are eligible. To qualify for one your disability must make walking difficult or impossible and must be likely to be permanent.

A MANUAL WHEELCHAIR will be supplied if your ability to walk is permanently restricted, whether you need one full-time or only occasionally.

A POWERED INDOOR WHEELCHAIR will be supplied only if your disability is so severe that you are unable to walk, unable to propel yourself indoors in a manual wheelchair and if it will give you some degree of independence.

A POWERED OUTDOOR WHEELCHAIR will be supplied only if you are unable to propel yourself indoors in a manual wheelchair AND if you rely on attendants who themselves are unable to push you in a wheelchair, due to the nature of the area and/or their own ability.

Buying a Wheelchair

POWERED WHEELCHAIRS are available in many different types: indoor, outdoor, attendant-controlled and self-controlled. They cost from £1,500. The batteries have to be replaced frequently too, which is another expense you should bear in mind if choosing a powered wheelchair. If you plan to use a heavier, outdoor type of powered wheelchair when travelling in a vehicle which has been adapted to take wheelchairs, you should check that the vehicle will be able to take your particular wheelchair. It may depend on the type of vehicle, tail-lift or ramp being used.

LARGER POWERED VEHICLES are also commercially available, ranging from three-wheeled scooters to 'buggies' with an enclosed cab. They can be driven on the pavement at up to 4 mph and some models can be driven into shops. They cost from £1,500 upwards. The majority have kerb-climbing ability, which is useful in areas where there are no dropped kerbs.

CLASS 3 "INVALID CARRIAGES" are outdoor powered vehicles with a maximum speed limit of 4 mph on pavements and other pedestrian areas, but can be driven on the road at up to 8 mph (they cannot be driven on motorways, in bus lanes or cycle lanes). Although you don't need a driving licence for these vehicles, you must understand the Highway Code if you intend to use one on the road. Training is available from the vehicle supplier, from the Royal Society for the Prevention of Accidents (RoSPA) or from your local authority's Road Safety Officer.

There are several guides to help you choose a wheelchair or electric vehicle:

- "Wheelchairs and their Use – A Guide to Choosing a Wheelchair". Available from RADAR;

- 'How To Choose A Pavement Vehicle". Available from the Banstead Mobility Centre;

- "Equipment For Disabled People – Wheelchairs". Available from the Disability Information Trust;

- "Choosing An Electric Wheelchair – Notes For Private Buyers". Available from DLF;

- "Manual Wheelchairs: List 14" *and*

- "Powered Wheelchairs: List 15". Both available from Disability Scotland;

- "8 mph Vehicles – Your Rights and Responsibilities". Available from the Department of Transport (DoT) Disability Unit.

Help with Buying a Powered Wheelchair or Electric Vehicle

If you receive DLA (Mobility Component) or War Pensioners' Mobility Supplement, you can put that towards the Motability Hire Purchase Scheme to buy either a powered wheelchair or a one-person electric vehicle. Motability will send you details on request. (Also see Chapter 6 "Cars and Driving".)

If you do not receive DLA (Mobility Component) or War Pensioners' Mobility Supplement, a voluntary organisation might be able to help you buy one. An alternative is to try to buy one second-hand through the 'small ads' columns of magazines for people with disabilities.

It is important to seek advice about buying a wheelchair and to try out wheelchairs before buying, whether new or second-hand.

Hiring a Wheelchair

If you need a wheelchair temporarily, you may be able to get one from your local authority's Social Services Department (Social Work Department in Scotland). Some Social Services Departments loan wheelchairs for short-term use such as holidays or whilst awaiting delivery of your own NHS one. You can rent a wheelchair from the British Red Cross Society (BRCS); for holidays the BRCS can arrange for a wheelchair to be waiting at your destination. Some branches of the Womens' Royal Voluntary Service (WRVS) will also hire out manual wheelchairs. Voluntary organisations usually make a small charge for such a loan.

Other firms which hire out wheelchairs can be found in the book "Motoring and Mobility for Disabled People", available from RADAR, or ask your local DLC.

Helping Wheelchair Users

Using a wheelchair to propel yourself requires training and practice; so too does pushing one. Both are described in **"How to Push a Wheelchair"**, available from the West Midlands Disabled Motorists Club. The BRCS produces a leaflet, **"People in Wheelchairs – Hints for Helpers"**.

▶ MOBILITY FOR BLIND AND PARTIALLY SIGHTED PEOPLE

Some local authorities employ specialist staff who can help blind and partially sighted people with mobility problems and teach them the skills to become independently mobile, if it is possible. Voluntary organisations may also be able to help in this way. Ask your local authority's Social Services Department (Social Work Department in Scotland) or contact the Royal National Institute for the Blind (RNIB). If you were blinded as a result of military service, St. Dunstan's or the Scottish National Institute for War Blinded can offer help and advice on many matters, including mobility and transport. If you are interested in owning a guide dog, you should contact the Guide Dogs for the Blind Association.

It is now possible to make raised tactile maps. There is a national register of areas which have been officially mapped. Social Services Departments or voluntary organisations may be able to provide a raised map for your area. Alternatively you can buy kits for making raised maps: contact the RNIB or your Social Services Department for details of stockists. RNIB will also make maps for you, for a fee. There are also spoken maps available for some areas.

Even if you are independently mobile, there are times when you may need to be guided by someone else, say at railway or bus stations. **"How to Guide a Blind Person"**, available from the RNIB, is a useful leaflet for those who help. They should also know that a red-and-white cane indicates that someone is deaf and blind, and that the National Deaf-Blind League publishes a leaflet on **"How to Talk to a Deaf-Blind Person"**. RNIB issues a leaflet on **"Helping People who are Deaf as Well as Blind**, and there is a car sticker which explains what a red-and-white cane means.

GETTING STARTED

Remember

- Make sure you are getting the benefit or allowance to which you are entitled.
- Getting the right benefit or allowance may mean you are able to afford the journeys you want or need to make.
- Getting the right equipment may mean you can make those journeys in much greater comfort.
- Entitlement to some benefits or local concessions may depend on being registered with your local authority as a disabled person.
- If you were not eligible for the old Mobility Allowance, you *may* now be eligible to receive DLA (Mobility Component) which has replaced it.
- If you think you are eligible for the DLA (Mobility Component) you must claim before your 66th birthday.
- There are DLCs throughout the country which you can visit to see and try out equipment to help you get around more easily.
- If you are going to get a wheelchair, think about where you want to use it, and get professional advice, before buying one.
- You do not have to buy a wheelchair. If you need one you can get it on permanent loan through the NHS.

▶ USEFUL CONTACTS

Age Concern England
1268 London Road
Norbury
London SW16 4ER
081–679 8000

Artificial Limb and Appliance Centre
Rookwood Hospital
Fairwater Road
Llandaff, Cardiff CF5 2YN
0222–555677

Banstead Mobility Centre
Damson Way, Orchard Hill
Queen Mary's Avenue
Carshalton, Surrey SM5 4NR
081–770 1151

British Red Cross Society (BRCS)
National Headquarters
9 Grosvenor Crescent
London SW1X 7EJ
071–235 5454

Citizens Advice Scotland
26 George Square
Edinburgh EH8 9LD
031–667 0156/7/8

Departments of Health and Social Security
(DH & DSS)
Leaflets Unit
PO Box 21
Stanmore, Middlesex HA7 1AY

DSS
Medical Devices Directorate
241 Bristol Ave
Bispham
Blackpool, Lancs. FY2 0BR
0253–596000

DSS
N9C (Invalid Vehicle Service)
Government Buildings
Warbreck Hill Road
Blackpool, Lancs. FY2 3TA
0253–856123

DSS
War Pensioners' Mobility Supplement
  Section
North Fylde Central Office
Norcross, Blackpool, Lancs. FY5 3TA
0253–856123

Department of Transport (DoT) Disability
  Unit
Room S10/21
2 Marsham Street
London SW1P 3EB
071–276 5257 (Minicom 071–276 4973)

The Disability Alliance (ERA)
Universal House
88–94 Wentworth Street
London E1 7SA
071–247 8776 (minicom available)

Disability Information Trust
Mary Marlborough Lodge
Nuffield Orthopaedic Centre
Oxford OX3 7LD
0865–750103

Disability Scotland
Princes House
5 Shandwick Place
Edinburgh EH2 4RG
031–229 8632

Disabled Living Centres Council
286 Camden Road
London N7 OBJ
071–700 1707

Disabled Living Foundation (DLF)
380–384 Harrow Road
London W9 2HU
071–289 6111

Disablement Income Group (DIG)
Millmead Business Centre
Millmead Road
London N17 9QU
081–801 8013

Disablement Income Group Scotland
5 Quayside Street
Leith, Edinburgh EH6 6EJ
031–555 2811

Disablement Information & Advice Line
  (DIAL) UK
Park Lodge, St. Catherine's Hospital
Tickhill Road
Balby, Doncaster, S. Yorks. DN4 8QN
0302–310123

Guide Dogs for the Blind Association
Hillfields
Burghfield Common, Reading, Berks. RG7
  3YG
0734–835555

Motability
2nd Floor, Gate House
West Gate, The High
Harlow, Essex CM20 1HR
0279–635666

National Association of Citizens Advice
  Bureaux
Myddleton House
115/123 Pentonville Road
London N1 9LZ
071–833 2181

National Deaf-Blind League
18 Rainbow Court
Paston Ridings
Peterborough PE4 7UP
0733–573511

Royal Association for Disability &
  Rehabilitation (RADAR)
25 Mortimer Street
London W1N 8AB
071–637 5400

Royal National Institute for the Blind
  (RNIB)
224 Great Portland Street
London W1N 6AA
071–388 1266

Royal Society for the Prevention of
  Accidents (RoSPA)
Cannon House
Priory Queensway
Birmingham B4 6BS
021–200 2461

St. Dunstan's
PO Box 4XB
12–14 Harcourt Street
London W1A 4XB
071–723 5021

Scottish Home & Health Department
  (SHHD)
St. Andrew's House
Regent Road
Edinburgh EH1 3DE
031–556 8400

Scottish National Institute for War Blinded
PO Box 500
Gillespie Crescent
Edinburgh EH10 4HZ
031–229 1456

Wales Council for the Disabled
Llys Ifor
Crescent Road
Caerphilly, Mid Glamorgan CF8 1XL
0222–887325/6/7

Welsh Office (WO)
LASS 1B
Cathays Park
Cardiff CF1 3NQ
0222–825111

West Midlands Disabled Motorists Club
Unit 2a, Atcham Industrial Estate
Upton Magna, Shrewsbury SY4 4UG
0743–761889

Womens' Royal Voluntary Service (WRVS)
Headquarters
234/244 Stockwell Road
London SW9 9SP
071–415 0146

2. PLANNING YOUR JOURNEY

▶ CHOOSING HOW TO GO

If you are making a journey for the first time, it can cause a great deal of anxiety, whether it is a local trip, long-distance, or involves travel abroad. If you have a mobility handicap that anxiety can be much greater. Sometimes you may even prefer not to make the journey at all. However, with the right preparations beforehand, your journey can be a stress-free experience, and often a pleasure in itself.

Access to transport is getting better all the time, with improvements to public transport, more voluntary transport schemes being set up and expanded, and private or commercial transport operators offering new or improved facilities for people with disabilities. Finding out what services and facilities exist can be a time-consuming business, and deciding how to make the journey can be frustrating, if you don't know where to get the right information and advice.

BUT THERE IS USUALLY HELP AT HAND.

Help with Travel and Transport Information

The following chapters give useful contacts for information about particular aspects of travel, or about particular areas where you may be travelling. But there are also organisations which can give you information and advice on the whole range of transport matters at home and abroad:

The Department of Transport, Disability Unit

This Unit is responsible for policy on transport for people with disabilities. It also deals with a wide range of queries, especially questions concerning transport legislation as it affects people with disabilities.

TRIPSCOPE

This a free travel and transport information service for disabled and elderly people. It is telephone based and can help with planning local, long-distance or international journeys, for whatever purpose, and can help with a wide range of transport questions.

In addition to these, you may be able to get useful information and advice from organisations which cater for the needs of people with specific disabilities. The names, addresses and telephone numbers of national disability organisations are listed in the Geographical Directory starting on page 113, under "Major National Disability and Voluntary Organisations".

General Information and Services

There are other organisations which offer information and advice on transport for people with disabilities or which represent the interests of travellers with mobility handicaps. However, many do not deal exclusively with this topic. They are more widely involved with either disability or transport matters.

Organisations Concerned with Transport for Disabled People

Disabled Persons' Transport Advisory Committee (DPTAC)

DPTAC considers any matter relating to the needs of people with disabilities in connection with transport. It gives advice to the Secretary of State for Transport on transport for people with disabilities.

Joint Committee on Mobility for Disabled People (JCMD)

This Committee represents and promotes all transport and mobility interests of physically disabled people.

Joint Committee on Mobility of Blind and Partially Sighted People (JCMBP)

This Committee represents and promotes all transport and mobility interests of visually impaired people.

Committee on Mobility for Scotland

The Committee represents and promotes all transport and mobility interests of disabled people.

Access to the Skies Committee

This Committee exists for information and improvements to airline travel for people with disabilities. It is mainly concerned with that part of the journey from check-in to baggage reclaim and promotes the improvement and development of facilities for disabled travellers.

Community Transport Association (CTA)

The Association runs training programmes, distributes publications, information and advice to organisations involved in the provision of community transport. It is also a 'Designated Body' entitled to issue 'Small Bus Permits' to its members. Whilst it is concerned with disability matters, it is more concerned with the wider issue of accessible transport provision for the whole community.

CTA Advice and Information

The Association also operates a separate service, giving free advice and information on all aspects of minibus and accessible transport operation.

Organisations Concerned Mainly with Transport Matters

Passenger Transport Executives (PTEs)

PTEs oversee public transport provision in six major metropolitan areas outside London, working to policies set by Passenger Transport Authorities for their areas. London Transport (LT) is the PTE for the London area. PTEs are responsible for passenger facilities and timetable information, as well as travel concessions for elderly, disabled and young people. The provision of specially designed services to meet the needs of disabled people is given a high priority.

Transport Users' Consultative Committees (TUCCs)

TUCCs are independent consumer bodies set up by Parliament to protect rail users' interests. They monitor the performance of British Rail (BR) in their areas and are able to make recommendations for changes. Their tasks include taking up passengers' complaints and considering objections to proposed line or station closures. (In London, the London Regional Passengers' Committee represents the interests of users of LT as well as BR.)

Air Transport Users' Committee (ATUC)

This Committee makes reports and recommendations to the Civil Aviation Authority for furthering the interests of air transport users, including investigation of complaints against air transport providers – airports, airlines, travel agents etc. They also produce two publications which are very useful for air travellers who have a disability: "Care In The Air – Advice For Handicapped Travellers" and "Flight Plan – Hints For Airline Passengers". They are both available from ATUC free of charge.

Organisations Concerned Mainly with Disability Issues

Access Committee for England
Access Committee for Wales
Scottish Committee on Access for Disabled People

These Committees promote access to buildings and the environment for people with sensory or physical disabilities by working with the Government, the private sector and local authorities, and by supporting Local Access Groups.

Royal Association for Disability and Rehabilitation (RADAR)

RADAR is a coordinating body for organisations serving disabled people. It also has a general information service.

Holiday Care Service

This is a voluntary organisation which can help with lots of useful information about holidays and holiday travel. It also produces a wide range of free information sheets.

Physically Handicapped and Able Bodied (PHAB)

PHAB is a coordinating body for clubs of physically handicapped and able bodied young people and adults.

► HELP FOR PEOPLE WITH HEARING IMPAIRMENTS

Sympathetic Hearing Scheme

A large number of railway stations, airports, bus stations and other public transport places have joined this scheme and display the international 'ear' symbol. The symbol indicates to people with hearing impairments that they will receive extra time and consideration at the establishments which display this sign.

If you have a hearing impairment you can join this scheme by applying to the British Association of the Hard of Hearing for a 'Sympathetic Hearing Scheme' card. You can use the card to obtain assistance where you see the symbol displayed, or to communicate with people on buses, trains or in the street. Full details will be sent to you on request.

Remember

● There are organisations which can help you plan your journey and answer any questions you may have.

● Disability organisations can often give useful information and advice about how best to cope with your own disability when travelling.

► USEFUL CONTACTS

Access Committee for England
35 Great Smith Street
London SW1P 3BJ
071–233 2566

Access Committee for Wales
c/o Wales Council for the Disabled
Llys Ifor
Crescent Road
Caerphilly, Mid Glamorgan
0222–887325

Access to the Skies Committee
c/o Secretary
RADAR, 25 Mortimer Street
London W1N 8AB
071–637 5400

Air Transport Users Committee (ATUC)
2nd Floor, Kingsway House
103 Kingsway
London WC2B 6QX
071–242 3882

Committee on Mobility for Scotland
Princes House
5 Shandwick Place
Edinburgh EH2 4RG
031–229 8632

Community Transport Association (CTA)
Highbank
Halton Street
Hyde, Cheshire SK14 2NY
061–351 1475 or 061–366 6685

Community Transport Association Advice &
 Information
061–367 8780

Department of Transport
Disability Unit
Room S10/21
2 Marsham Street
London SW1P 3EB
071–276 5257 (Minicom 071-276 4973)

Disabled Persons Transport Advisory
    Committee (DPTAC)
Secretariat: Room S10/21
Department of Transport
2 Marsham Street
London SW1P 3EB
071–276 5257 (Minicom 071-276 4973)

Holiday Care Service
2 Old Bank Chambers
Station Road
Horley, Surrey RH6 9HW
0293–77455

Joint Committee on Mobility of Blind and
    Partially Sighted People (JCMBP)
224 Great Portland Street
London W1N 6AA
071–388 1266

Joint Committee on Mobility for Disabled
    People (JCMD)
The Secretary
Woodcliff House
51a Cliff Road
Weston-Super-Mare, Avon BS22 9SE
0934–642313

British Association of the Hard of Hearing
7–11 Armstrong Road
London W3 7JL
081–743 1110

Physically Handicapped and Able Bodied
    (PHAB)
12–14 London Road
Croydon CR0 2TA
081–667 9443

Royal Association for Disability and
    Rehabilitation (RADAR)
25 Mortimer Street
London W1N 8AB
071–637 5400

Scottish Committee on Access for Disabled
    People
c/o Disability Scotland
5 Shandwick Place
Edinburgh EH2 4RG
031–229 8632

TRIPSCOPE
63 Esmond Road
London W4 1JE
081–994 9294 (Minicom available)

and

Pamwell House
160 Pennywell Road
Bristol BS5 0TX
0272–414094

Passenger Transport Executives (PTEs)

Greater Manchester Passenger Transport
    Executive
Magnum House
9 Portland Street, Piccadilly Gardens
Manchester M60 1HX
061–228 6400

South Yorkshire Passenger Transport
    Executive
Exchange Street
Sheffield S2 5SZ
0742–767575
0742–768688 (Traveline)

Strathclyde Passenger Transport Executive
Consort House
12 West George Street
Glasgow G2 1HN
041–332 6811

Tyne & Wear Passenger Transport Executive
Cuthbert House
All Saints Centre
Newcastle-upon-Tyne NE1 2DA
091–261 0431

Centro
(West Midlands Passenger Transport
    Executive)
Commercial Department
16 Summer Lane
Birmingham B19 3SD
021–200 2787

West Yorkshire Passenger Transport
  Executive
Wellington House
40–50 Wellington Street
Leeds LS1 2DE
0532–440988

County Councils

For County Council public transport contacts
  see Appendix A.

Transport Users Consultative Committees (TUCCs)

England

Central Transport Consultative Committee
1st Floor, Golden Cross House
8 Duncannon Street
London WC2N 4JF
071–839 7338

Eastern England:
TUCC for Eastern England
Midgate House, Midgate
Peterborough PE1 1TN
0783–312188

North Western England:
TUCC for North Western England
Room 112, Boulton House
17–21 Chorlton Street
Manchester M1 3HY
061–228 6247

North Eastern England:
TUCC for North Eastern England
Hilary House
16 St. Saviour's Place
York YO1 2PL
0904–625615

Southern England:
TUCC for Southern England
Room 218–220, Golden Cross House
8 Duncannon Street
London WC2N 4JF
071–839 1851/2

Western England:
TUCC for Western England
13th Floor, Tower House
Fairfax Street
Bristol BS1 3BN
0272–265703

The Midlands:
TUCC for the Midlands
77 Paradise Circus
Queensway
Birmingham B1 2DT
021–212 2133

London:
London Regional Passengers Committee
  (LRPC)
2nd Floor, Golden Cross House
8 Duncannon Street
London WC2N 4JF
071–839 1898/9

Scotland

TUCC for Scotland
249 West George Street
Glasgow G2 4QE
041–221 7760

Wales

TUCC for Wales
St. David's House, East Wing
Wood Street
Cardiff CF1 1ES
0222–227247

3. LOCAL TRIPS

If you are living in, or visiting, London you can also find information about making local trips there in Chapter 4 "Travelling In And Across London"

CONTENTS   PAGE NO.

▶ CHOOSING HOW TO GO

Usually it is trips to local destinations which you want to make most often. In choosing what transport to use you should think about the reason for your trip, as well as your degree of mobility. Of course your choice may depend above all on what transport is actually available where you live.

There is often more than one way of making the trip and it is worth thinking about what suits you best: special door-to-door (w) accessible minibus, taxi, local bus, metro? The cost is an important consideration: what concessions are available, or is there any other sort of help with the fare?

To help you decide, and to find out what transport is available with any special facilities for people with disabilities, you can contact your County Council Public Transport Information Officer. Some counties also publish a guide to transport facilities in the county for elderly or disabled people (see the panel on page 28 for a full list). Many local authorities publish local area access guides. A full list is available from the Royal Association for Disability and Rehabilitation (RADAR). Your local Disablement Information and Advice Line (DIAL) would also know if one is available for your area.

For travel in Northern Ireland you should contact Disability Action (formerly the Northern Ireland Council on Disability), which publishes "On the Move", a guide to mobility in Northern Ireland.

▶ BUSES

Travelling by Bus

At some of the busier bus stops you may find shelters and seats, but not always. You can check with your local bus company. You can usually get details of facilities at bus stations, including toilet and refreshment arrangements, from the local access guide, if there is one for your area.

If you have difficulty in walking, climbing or holding, you will find that modern buses generally have lower steps, better handholds throughout the vehicle, non-slip floors and better lighting. Many now have easier-to-use bell pushes and 'bus stopping' signs that light up to show you that the driver will stop at the next bus stop so you do not need to hurry from your seat. Most buses also have seats near the entrance reserved for disabled and elderly people.

Travelling By Bus In Your Wheelchair

If you are able to transfer from your wheelchair, it will still be difficult using ordinary buses. Getting a folded wheelchair on board is difficult unless you have someone with you who can help (and you are fairly agile yourself). Some operators provide special help for people in wheelchairs to use ordinary services if arrangements can be made in advance. Your Public Transport Information Officer would know if such help is available in your area.

If you need to travel in your wheelchair, there are increasing numbers of services operated with specially adapted buses. They have passenger lifts and staff who are trained to be aware of the needs of people with disabilities (but these buses are not *exclusively* for the use of disabled people, anyone can use them).

These services are generally available only in the larger towns and cities and operate a different route each day of the week between residential areas and the main shoppping centre, hospital, etc. Again, the Public Transport Information Officer for your area would know where these bus services run.

Help Available

Few buses now have conductors. Drivers are usually not allowed to leave their cab to help you on or off the bus, but training schemes have been introduced to make them aware of the needs of people with disabilities. So, for example, don't hesitate to ask the driver to let you get to a seat before the bus starts off.

A few bus operators also run 'Helping Hand' schemes where volunteer helpers are available to help people with disabilities. Your Public Transport Information Officer should be able to let you know if there are any of these schemes in your area. The amount of help available varies: some provide escorts for people who have to be accompanied door-to-door; others just supply help in getting on or off the bus.

Help for Blind and Partially Sighted People

The Royal National Institute for the Blind (RNIB) can supply blind and partially sighted people with large-print numbered cards to use at bus stops. The RNIB has also produced a free fluorescent 'BUS' card for blind people to use at bus stops. This is useful for 'Hail and Ride' services. You should ask the driver to tell you where and when to get off the bus.

Help for Passengers with Hearing and Speech Impairments

In some areas of the country 'Helping Hand' forms have been introduced. You can fill in details of your journey and hand it to the driver when you get on the bus. The forms are especially useful if you have speech or hearing problems or if you have learning difficulties. You can usually get the forms from local bus operators and local disability organisations.

The Stroke Association has produced a plastic identity card for people with a speech impairment to use when travelling. The international 'ear' symbol is used on some buses and at travel information offices to indicate that staff understand the problems of people who are hard of hearing.

Post Buses

Post Buses carry passengers as well as delivering and collecting mail. The vehicles used are large estate cars, Land Rovers or minibuses and they run on a published route and to a timetable. They can provide a valuable transport service for people with disabilities in rural areas, especially in Scotland, where there may be no other public transport. Whilst most are not (w) accessible, the service in Sittingbourne, Kent is operated with a (w) accessible vehicle, and further (w) accessible routes are planned. You can get a list of services operated by Post Buses from The Post Office Public Affairs Departments in London or Edinburgh, or from the National Post Bus Development Manager.

▶ UNDERGROUND AND METRO

The older underground railway systems are generally less accessible than the newer metro or light rail transport systems which have recently come into operation or are currently being planned and built. These new railways are generally fully (w) accessible, whether they are using older British Rail (BR) stations in the suburbs, or new city centre stations. In each case you can get more information from the Information Centre for the Passenger Transport Executive (PTE) responsible. (See Chapter 2, "Getting Started", for a list of PTEs.)

Glasgow Underground

Although the system has been modernised it is not (w) accessible. However, facilities are good for those who do not need to travel in a wheelchair.

Manchester Metrolink

All the stations and a section of each train are fully (w) accessible. The first phase covers the route from Bury in the north to Altrincham in the south, via Central Manchester and both Victoria and Piccadilly BR stations, and began operating in April 1992. Running on former BR tracks in the suburbs, the trains will run on new street-level tracks through the City centre.

Merseyrail Underground

The trains are (w) accessible with wide doors, although suburban stations can be difficult for wheelchair users. New stations have ramped access to the platforms and access is being improved at older stations. Lifts are provided for people with disabilities at stations in central Liverpool and Birkenhead.

Tyne and Wear Metro

This system was also designed to be fully accessible to all people with disabilities. There are specially designed interchanges with links to bus stations and with parking spaces reserved for people with disabilities.

▶ LOCAL RAIL SERVICES

BR staff will do all they can to help, but you should give advance notice so that the right help can be made available. This can be arranged in advance through the special 'Assistance' phone line in each Local Manager's office (see page 63 for details). They are also listed in a useful leaflet, "British Rail and Disabled Travellers", available from stations and Travel Centres.

Access at many suburban stations involves stairs and a bridge or subway to reach the platform. Ramps or a lift are usually available at the larger mainline stations and BR has many 'Core Stations' throughout the country which are fully (w) accessible, so it may be better to start or finish your rail journey at one of the more accessible stations, even if this involves a longer road journey to or from the station. You need to bear in mind also that **some stations are unstaffed all the time and there will be no one there to help you, whilst others are staffed only part of the time.** You should check with your local manager whether there will be help available at the station when you want to travel (AND when you want to return!).

More modern trains have wide sliding doors, operated by push-buttons on either side of the door (people of restricted growth may have some difficulty reaching the buttons). These trains have low floors, grabrails, roomy vestibules and plenty of space for passengers in wheelchairs. Older trains have narrow doors, and if you need to travel in a wheelchair you will have to travel in the guard's van.

You can get more details on access at stations and to trains from your BR local manager (see page 63).

Help for Passengers with Hearing or Speech Impairments

All stations normally display printed timetables or departure sheets and most local trains show their destination above the front window.

▶ TAXIS AND PRIVATE HIRE

Taxis and private hire cars can be booked in advance to give you a door-to-door service, wherever you want to go, but licensed taxis can also be hired at a taxi-rank or in the street. Outside London, many taxis and hire cars are large saloon or estate cars. These are not (w) accessible, but if you can transfer from your wheelchair, most can take a folded wheelchair in the boot.

Wheelchair Accessible Taxis

Some taxi companies have adapted minibuses which can be hired, but these will be more expensive than ordinary taxis. In London all new taxis are (w) accessible and elsewhere in the country many councils are now insisting that new licences will only be given to taxis if

LOCAL TRIPS

these are (w) accessible. This generally means the 'Fairway' or 'Metrocab', the most modern versions of London's traditional black cabs. You can find out whether any of these are operating in your area by contacting the taxi licensing office of your district, borough or city council.

London-style Taxi or Saloon Car?

If you need to travel in a wheelchair the (w) accessible taxi is an obvious choice, where it is available. If you find stepping up into a London-style taxi too difficult you may prefer to use a taxi company which still uses saloon cars; however, all new models of the 'Fairway' London-style taxi are fitted with an extra step and a swivel seat so you can sit down before swinging round into the taxi.

Whichever type of taxi you choose, the driver will usually help you in and out of the taxi if you ask.

Help for Blind and Partially Sighted People

The RNIB has produced a 'TAXI' sign to help blind and partially sighted people hail a taxi.

Help with Fares

The cost of this door-to-door service is more than going by public transport. As the taxi fare is based on the length of your journey, taxis are best used for short distances or special occasions (eg: when you have a lot of luggage or shopping and the convenience outweighs the cost). However, if there are two or more of you travelling, the cost can be shared to make the outlay much more reasonable.

Many councils issue concessionary tokens or vouchers for use on public transport and sometimes these can be used towards the cost of a local taxi fare. You should contact your County Council Public Transport Information Officer or Social Services Department to find out whether the tokens or vouchers can be used for taxi trips in your area. In some areas there are **Taxicard** schemes for disabled residents who cannot use ordinary public transport. These schemes allow their members to make local taxi trips for a much reduced fare. They operate in London (see page 46 for further details), Tyne & Wear, Cambridge and Plymouth in England and in the following Regions of Scotland: Central, Grampian, Lothian and Tayside. For further information you should contact your local authority (or the appropriate regional council in Scotland). See the main geographical directory at Appendix A for addresses and telephone numbers.

▶ **VOLUNTARY ORGANISATIONS**

If you have no transport of your own and you have a mobility handicap which prevents you using ordinary buses and trains, there are many voluntary organisations which can help with local (and sometimes longer distance) trips, whatever the reason for your trip, and whatever your degree of mobility. These door-to-door transport services are usually operated by helpful, specially trained staff and can bring you independence of travel at a reasonable price.

In many rural areas with no frequent bus or train services, these local transport schemes may be the only way of getting out and about if you do not have access to a car.

The schemes vary from those operated with ordinary cars to those run with (w) adapted minibuses. You usually have to book in advance and make a payment based on the mileage, or give a donation. Most locally-based schemes will only take you on trips within your local area, but some will take you further afield, although the cost for this will naturally be greater.

For longer-distance journeys it may be better – and it is usually cheaper – to use a local voluntary transport scheme to take you to a bus, coach or railway station to link up with coach or rail services. See Chapter 5 "Travelling Further Afield" for more details.

Community Transport

Local Community Transport (CT) organisations usually have a pool of vehicles which they will hire out to local member groups or associations, with or without a driver depending on the particular CT group. If your own group wants to hire a vehicle and supply its own driver, he or she will usually be required to meet certain conditions and take a familiarisation test.

The vehicles are generally, but not always, (w) accessible and can be hired by most local community groups including disability organisations. Some CT organisations run Social Car Schemes and provide other services for disabled people (eg: furniture removal) as well. To find out whether there is a CT organisation in your area you should contact the Community Transport Association. The Department of Transport (DoT) can supply a "Directory of Voluntary and Community Transport", covering either the whole country or on a county-by-county basis. It is available free of charge from the Disability Unit at the DoT.

Dial-a-Ride

Most large urban areas and many small towns now have a door-to-door transport service especially for people who are unable to use public transport. They are known by a variety of names besides Dial-a-Ride (Ring-and-Ride, Dial-a-Journey etc.) but essentially they all provide the same type of service specially designed to meet your individual needs:

- Specially adapted (w) accessible minibuses or cars are used.
- Staff are specially trained and helpful.
- The service is door-to-door.
- The service usually operates 7 days a week from early morning to late evening.
- The bus comes to your home and takes you where you want to go: shops, visiting friends, social events.
- You will not be able to use the service for trips to hospital for medical treatment or for other journeys where local or health authority transport is available.
- You have to book in advance but you can arrange your return booking at the same time.
- Fares are usually based on local bus fares.
- Concessionary passes are sometimes accepted.
- The service is usually only for local residents who have to register, but some dial-a-rides will assist visitors if possible.
- Most services will only take you on trips in the local area where they are based.

Some dial-a-ride services are run by the local CT organisation. To find out whether there is a local dial-a-ride service in your area you should contact the CTA, the Public Transport Information Officer in your county council or your local Social Services Department.

Women's Safe Transport

In some areas special transport schemes are run in the evenings for women, by women. Some of the vehicles used are (w) accessible as the schemes are usually attached to the local CT organisation. The schemes are generally run in the same way as dial-a-rides. To find out if there is a scheme run with (w) accessible vehicles in your area you should contact your borough or district council, which would usually fund the schemes).

Social Car Schemes

Some organisations run Social Car Schemes with volunteer drivers. The volunteers use their own cars to drive people who cannot use public transport, mainly on local trips, but some will travel longer distances. There is a charge, based on the distance involved (remember it will include the 'empty' return journey for the driver as well). Some schemes will only take you to hospital appointments, to doctors' surgeries, or to collect prescriptions; others will take you anywhere you want to go.

The schemes are run by a variety of organisations:

- *local Volunteer Bureaux or local Voluntary Services Councils* (although NOT ALL run transport schemes). Check with your local transport guide if your county council publishes one (see the panel on page 28), or with your local Citizens Advice Bureau for futher information.

- *local authority Social Services Departments (Social Work Departments in Scotland)* – a very few run Social Car Schemes with volunteer drivers.

- *CT Organisations* – some run a Social Car Scheme.

- *Womens' Royal Voluntary Service (WRVS)* – mainly for health or welfare purposes. (They do not supply transport in the London area.) Sometimes the Social Car Scheme is run by them for the county council.

- *The British Red Cross Society (BRCS)*

If you need (w) accessible transport this can be provided with the ambulances of the BRCS or St. John Ambulance but the cost of the journey will be higher. Some WRVS local groups also run minibuses fitted with a lift to take you in your wheelchair, mainly for shopping.

Other Voluntary Organisations

Many disability groups and other organisations such as Age Concern, Multiple Sclerosis Society branches and PHAB clubs have (w) accessible minibuses for taking their own members on outings, to social events, etc. Usually they are for the exclusive use of their own members, but some groups do make their vehicles available to other organisations, or will take you as a passenger, with their own driver. You should check with the individual local group to find out whether such hiring is possible.

Escorts

If you are travelling alone and need someone to go with you, escorts can be provided by WRVS and BRCS. Of course, their fares to and from home and expenses (meals on a long journey) will have to be paid. BRCS supplies trained escorts, but the WRVS escorts are not medically qualified and cannot offer nursing care on the journey.

▶ TRANSPORT FOR PARTICULAR TRIPS

Help can be available if you need to make a trip for a particular reason.

Going Shopping: Shopmobility Schemes

Many towns have large pedestrianised shopping areas and a growing number of 'Shopmobility' schemes have been set up to give people with disabilities the maximum mobility when shopping there. The panel on page 32 lists the towns where there are already Shopmobility schemes operating, their location and a telephone number for detailed information on what help can be provided, the times it is available, etc. Do telephone first, as these vary from town to town.

Powered and manual wheelchairs, as well as electric scooters, are available on loan. If enough advance notice is given an escort can often be provided to help with shopping, particularly useful if you are visually impaired. The wheelchairs and scooters are usually provided free, but you should be prepared to give proof of your identity. Sometimes a returnable nominal deposit is required, or you may have to leave your car parking ticket or car keys at the office until you return the wheelchair or scooter.

If you do not have access to a car and cannot use public transport, you may find that your local Shopmobility scheme ties up with your local dial-a-ride or CT scheme so that transport to and from the shopping area can be arranged as well.

Some local authority Social Services Departments (Social Work Departments in Scotland) have volunteer drivers who can help with essential shopping.

Going to Work

If you do not have your own car, finding suitable transport to and from work on a regular basis can be a problem, especially if it has to be (w) accessible. You usually cannot book the transport provided by voluntary organisations on a regular, long-term basis and (w) accessible public transport may not run close enough to your home and place of work at the times you need it.

If your journey to and from work is not too long, a taxi or hire car may be the answer; their door-to-door service can be booked ahead on a regular long-term basis. If there is a taxicard scheme in your area this may make the cost of travelling regularly by taxi affordable. However, taxicard schemes are increasingly limiting the number of trips you can make and you may wish to save these for other trips.

BUT there is still a way of getting help with fares to work by taxi:

> The Employment Service will pay towards taxi fares to work if you are severely disabled, on the Disabled Persons' Employment Register, and paying extra travell-

ing costs because you cannot use public transport for your journey to and from work. If you have your own car you can still get help with taxi fares to work if your car is out of service.

The Employment Service will pay three-quarters of the total cost of your journeys to and from work by taxi or hire car, up to a maximum of £87.50 (December 1991) for a 5-day week.

If you get the new Disability Living Allowance or the Disability Working Allowance (instead of the old Mobility Allowance) the amount you receive in support will be reduced to two-thirds of the total cost, up to a maximum of £77.75.

There are a number of special exceptions and you can get more details from the Disablement Resettlement Officer (DRO) at your local Jobcentre or Employment Office (look under 'Employment' in the Business section of your telephone book), but do get estimates of the cost from three different taxi companies first.

Going to Day Centres: Local Authority Transport

Local authority transport is usually provided in vehicles fitted with lifts, to take passengers in wheelchairs. Social Services Departments of the county, district or borough councils (in England and Wales) and Social Work Departments of the regional or islands councils (in Scotland) provide door-to-door transport, usually for groups of people with disabilities using local authority services – especially going to and from day centres. Sometimes there is a small charge.

The vehicles used are sometimes available for other social services or essential journey purposes, and during the evenings or weekends may be available for hire or loan to voluntary organisations offering a related service.

Going to Hospital

For Treatment

If you need to go to hospital for out-patient treatment, you may be able to go by ambulance. Your doctor will have to authorise this, normally at least a day ahead of the appointment. If you need to travel in a wheelchair, you may be able to travel in the ambulance in your wheelchair, provided you give enough notice so that a suitable vehicle can be arranged. Some older ambulances may not have the facilities to take you safely in a wheelchair.

If it is not necessary to travel in an ambulance, the ambulance service may well provide a car instead.

If you do not qualify on medical grounds for ambulance service transport to and from hospital, you may be able to get help with travelling expenses if:

- you are on Income Support; OR
- you receive Family Credit; OR
- you receive a War or MOD Disablement Pension; OR
- you live in the Isles of Scilly and have to travel to the mainland to hospital; OR

- you live in the area covered by the Scottish Highland and Islands Development Board and have to travel beyond a certain distance; OR
- you generally have a low income.

The Department of Social Service (DSS) provides a leaflet H11, "NHS Hospital Travel Costs", available free from your local DSS office. In the Scottish Highlands and Islands Development Board area you should contact the Scottish Home and Health Department (SHHD).

To Visit Someone

If you are visiting someone in hospital you should be able to get transport from one of the voluntary organisations already referred to on page 22. If you cannot afford the fares to and from hospital you may be able to get help with the fares if:

- you are visiting a close relative AND
  you receive Income Support; OR
- you are visiting a War or MOD Disabled Pensioner who is being treated for the disability to which the pension relates.

More information is available in the DSS leaflet H11 referred to in the previous section.

Going to School or College

Transport is provided by your local authority for disabled children and young people to get to and from school, whether or not it is a special school. Usually there are no restrictions on the distance. The transport used may be a local authority bus or a local taxi or hire car.

If you want to take up further, higher or continuing education once you leave school, and need help with transport, you should contact your Local Authority Education Department. The National Bureau for Students with Disabilities (SKILL) may also be able to give some advice on transport matters.

▶ CONCESSIONS

Help with the cost of taxi fares has already been mentioned under "Taxis and Private Hire", page 21 and "Going to Work", page 25. Concessionary fares are often available for disabled and elderly people on buses and trains (see page 47 for details of concessionary fares available in London for London residents).

In England and Wales your county or district council decides whether to offer concessions on public transport. In Scotland it is up to the regional and islands councils. The situation varies between:

- no concessions at all;
- reduced fare concessions outside peak hours;
- free travel outside peak hours.

LOCAL TRIPS

Schemes take the form of either tokens for disabled/elderly travellers to put towards the cost of public transport (sometimes including taxi fares) or passes entitling the holder to free or cheaper travel.

It is up to your local council to decide whether you qualify for concessionary travel, but the schemes usually include people over pensionable age and registered blind people (guide dogs always travel free). To find out whether there is a concessionary fare scheme in your area, you should contact your County Council Public Transport Information Officer or your local PTE.

Railway users who are disabled can also get a Disabled Person's Railcard, which gives substantial discounts on rail tickets. (People who have to travel in their wheelchairs can also get discounts on rail travel, whether or not they hold a Disabled Person's Railcard.) More details about these are given in Chapter 5 "Travelling Further Afield".

Remember

- Many county councils publish local transport guides for people with disabilities.
- Public Transport Information Officers in your county council can tell you about any special services, facilities or concessions available.
- Buses are becoming less of a problem as newer vehicles are designed to be easier to use.
- Taxis need not always be expensive, especially if you can share your trips with someone else.
- Transport run by voluntary organisations such as Dial-a-Ride gives you door-to-door travel with trained and helpful staff.
- If there is a special reason for your trip, there may be a scheme to help with the transport.

▶ **COUNTY GUIDES**

A number of guides is available which give useful information on local transport for people with a mobility handicap. They are free of charge and usually (but not always) published by the county council (regional council in Scotland) or Passenger Transport Executive (PTE). As at April 1992 they are available for the following areas:

COUNTY	PUBLISHED BY/AVAILABLE FROM
Bedfordshire	
Survival Guide For People With Physical Disabilities	Dominique Joyeux 67 Phillpotts Avenue, Bedford MK40 3UE; *or* tel. Pat Titmus: 0234–271087

COUNTY	PUBLISHED BY/AVAILABLE FROM
Buckinghamshire	
Mobility Guide For Buckinghamshire	Council for Voluntary Service Walton House, Walton Street Aylesbury, Bucks, HP21 7QQ 0296–21036
Alternative Transport Schemes – A guide to Alternative and Voluntary Transport Schemes in Buckinghamshire	Bucks. Council for Voluntary Service (see above), *or* Bucks. County Council, Passenger Transport Office, County Hall, Aylesbury, Bucks. HP20 1YZ 0296–382000
Cheshire	
Getting There – A Guide to Public Transport for People With a Mobility Problem	Cheshire County Council Transport Coordination Backford Hall, nr Chester CH1 6QA 0244–603742 (Cathy Cansdale)
Cumbria	
Directory Of Voluntary Transport Provision In Cumbria	Cumbria Transport Forum Andrew Beeforth c/o Volunteer Bureau 102 Highgate, Kendal Cumbria LA9 4HE 0539–729168
Derbyshire	
Going Places – A Guide to Transport Facilities for Disabled People in Derbyshire	Derbyshire County Council Public Transport Unit County Offices, Matlock Derbyshire DE4 3AG 0629–580000 ext. 6741
Devon	
A Guide To Transport Services In Devon – with particular reference to rural communities, elderly and disabled people.	Devon County Council, Public Transport, County Hall, Topsham Road Exeter, Devon EX2 4QR 0392–382123 (Karen Whatley)
Durham	
Guide to be published during 1992	Public Transport and Environment Department Durham County Council County Hall, Durham DH1 5UQ 091–386 4411 ext.2212

LOCAL TRIPS

COUNTY	PUBLISHED BY/AVAILABLE FROM
Essex	
A Guide To Welfare Transport In Essex – Appendix 11 of the latest Public Transport Plan	Planning Department, Essex County Council Public Transport Branch County Hall Chelmsford, Essex CM1 1LF 0245–492211
Gloucestershire	
Travel Guide – with special reference to travel for elderly and disabled people	Public Transport Manager Gloucestershire County Council Shire Hall, Bearland, Gloucester GL1 2TH 0452–425609
Hampshire	
Getting About In Hampshire A Travel Guide for Disabled and Elderly People	Passenger Transport Group County Surveyor's Department Hampshire County Council The Castle, Winchester Hants. SO23 8UD 0962–846983
Hertfordshire	
New guide being published during 1992	Passenger Transport Unit The Trinity Centre Fanhams Hall Road, Ware Herts. SG12 7LU 0992–588172 (Lindsay Walker)
Kent	
Transport Directory For The Mobility Impaired	Kent County Council Highways & Transportation Sandling Block, Springfield Maidstone, Kent ME14 2LQ 0622–671411
Lancashire	
Around Lancashire By Rail – A Guide to Station Facilities for Persons with Mobility Difficulties	Lancashire County Council County Surveyors Department Transport Coordination Section PO Box 9, Winckley House Cross Street Preston PR1 8RD 0772–264582/3

COUNTY	PUBLISHED BY/AVAILABLE FROM
Leicestershire	
Directory Of Groups And Organisations With Transport For Elderly And Disabled People In Leicestershire	D.I.A.L. Leicester 76 Clarendon Park Road Leicester LE2 3AD
Lincolnshire	
Guide to be published during 1992	County Transport Agency Highways & Planning Department Lincolnshire County Council City Hall, Beaumont Fee Lincoln LN1 1DN 0522–553132
Oxfordshire	
A Directory Of Rural Transport Schemes	Transport Officer Oxfordshire Rural Community Council, The Hadow Rooms 101 Banbury Road Oxford OX2 6NE 0865–512488 (Irene Reveco)
Surrey	
Community Transport Register	Surrey Voluntary Service Council, Astolat, Coniers Way New Inn Lane, Burtham Guildford, Surrey GU4 7HL 0483–66072 (Wendy Webb or Wendy Allison).
Access Bus – Transport For The Community	Surrey County Council Transportation Planning Unit, County Hall Kingston-Upon-Thames Surrey KT1 2DN 081–541 9482
West Midlands	
Getting Around – A Guide for People with a Mobility Problem in the West Midlands (also on cassette)	Centro, 16 Summer Lane Birmingham B19 3SD 021–200 2700 (B'ham area) 0203–559559 (Coventry area)

LOCAL TRIPS

COUNTY	PUBLISHED BY / AVAILABLE FROM
Wiltshire	
Directory Of Wiltshire Community Transport Schemes And Of Transport Facilities For The Elderly And Disabled	Transport Broker Department of Planning and Highways, County Hall Trowbridge, Wilts. BA14 8JD 0225–753641 ext. 3454 (T. Bellenger)
SCOTLAND	
Transport Information And Regulations *Directory Of Transport In Scotland*	Disability Scotland Princes House 5 Shandwick Place Edinburgh EH2 4RG 031–229 8632
Lothian	
Transport In Lothian	Lothian Regional Council 24 St Giles Street Edinburgh EH1 1PT 031–225 3858
Tayside	
Guide to be published during 1992	Transport Unit Roads & Transport Department Tayside Regional Council Parker Street Dundee DD1 5RW 0382–303006

▶ **TOWNS WITH SHOPMOBILITY SCHEMES**

TOWN AND ADDRESS	TELEPHONE NUMBER FOR FURTHER INFORMATION
NATIONAL FEDERATION OF SHOPMOBILITY	
The Secretary 26 Stanley Drive, Leicester LE5 1EA	0533–526604
ENGLAND	
Basildon	
103A Lower Galleries Eastgate Centre, Basildon, Essex SS14 1AG	0268–533644

TOWN AND ADDRESS	TELEPHONE NUMBER FOR FURTHER INFORMATION
Bassetlaw	
The Priory Centre, off Bridge Place Worksop, Nottinghamshire	0909–479070
Bexleyheath	
1st Floor, Norwich Place End Broadway Shopping Centre, Bexleyheath, Kent	081–301 5237
Bradford	
John Street Market, Rawson Road Bradford, West Yorkshire	0274–754076
Braintree	
First Stop Centre, Town Hall Annexe Fairfield Road, Braintree, Essex CM7 6HF	0376–46535
Brierly-hill	
Information Desk, Merryhill Shopping Centre Brierly-hill, West Midlands DY5 1SY	0384–481141
Cambridge	
Level 9, Lion Yard Car Park, Cambridge (Write to: Engineers Dept. Cambridge City Council, The Guildhall, Cambridge)	0223–463370
Chesterfield	
Gr. flr. Multi-storey Car Park, New Beetwell St. Chesterfield, Derbyshire S40 1QR	0246–209668
Colchester	
15 Queen Street, Colchester, Essex CO1 2PH	0206–369099
Dartford	
Priory Shopping Centre Dartford, Kent DA1 2HS	0322–220915
Derby	
The Bold Lane Car Park Bold Lane, Derby	0332–200320
Dewsbury	
Dewsbury Day Centre, Town Hall Way Railway Street, Dewsbury, W. Yorkshire	0924–455149
Gateshead	
Bus Station Office, The Metro Centre Gateshead, Tyne & Wear, NE11 9YG	091–460 5299

LOCAL TRIPS

TOWN AND ADDRESS	TELEPHONE NUMBER FOR FURTHER INFORMATION
Gloucester	
Hampden Car Park, Hampden Way, Gloucester (Write to: The Herbert Warehouse, The Docks, Gloucester, GL1 2EQ)	0452–396898
Harlow	
Post Office Car Park, Harlow, Essex CM20 1AA	0279–446188
Hatfield	
98 Town Centre, The Commons Hatfield, Herts. AL10 0NG	0707–262731
Hereford	
Maylord Orchards Car Park, Blueschool St. Hereford, Hereford & Worcester HR4 9EU	0432–342166
Huddersfield	
Disability Services, The Day Centre, Zetland St., Huddersfield, West Yorks. HD1 2RA	0484–453000
Ipswich	
Upper Barclay Street, Ipswich, Suffolk	0473–222225
Keighley	
Cooke Street, Keighley, West Yorkshire	0274–758225
Kingston-upon-Thames	
Eden Walk Car Park, Union Street Kingston-upon-Thames, Surrey KT1 1BL	081–547 1255
Leicester	
Gr. Flr. Newark Street Car Park (nr. the Phoenix) Leicester LE1 6ZG	0533–526694
Lincoln	
Tentercroft St. Car Park, Lincoln	0522–544983 (Lincoln Dial-a-Ride)
Luton	
Level 3, Market Car Park, Melson Street Luton, Bedfordshire	0582–412636

TOWN AND ADDRESS	TELEPHONE NUMBER FOR FURTHER INFORMATION
Milton Keynes	
Shopping Information Centre Midsummer Arcade, Secklow Gate West, Milton Keynes, Bucks. MK9 3ES	0908–670866
Northampton	
Greyfriars Car Park, Greyfriars, Northampton (Write to: 13 Hazlewood Rd, Northampton NN1 1LG)	0604–233714
Nottingham	
St Nicholas Centre, Stanford St. Nottingham NG1 6AE	0602–584486
Peterborough	
Level 11, Queensgate Car Park, Queensgate Centre, Peterborough, Cambs. PE1 1NT	0733–313133
Plymouth	
Charles Cross Car Park, City Centre, Plymouth, Devon PL1 1AT	0752–600633
Preston	
Mobility Centre, 28 Friargate, Preston, Lancs. PR1 3NN	0772–204667
Redditch	
Car Park 3, Access 3, Kingfisher Centre, Redditch, Hereford & Worcester	0527–69922
Sandwell	
Gr. Flr. Multi-storey Car Park Sandwell Shopping Centre, West Bromwich, West Midlands B70 7NJ	021–553 1943
Southend-on-Sea	
Farrington Car Park, off Elmer Approach, Southend-on-Sea, Essex	0702–339682
Sutton	
Gibson Road Car Park, Sutton, Surrey	081–770 0691
Sutton Coldfield	
Gracechurch Shopping Centre, Sutton Coldfield, West Midlands B72 1PH	021–355 1112

LOCAL TRIPS

TOWN AND ADDRESS	TELEPHONE NUMBER FOR FURTHER INFORMATION
Telford	
Information Centre, Piccadilly Square Telford Shopping Centre Telford, Shropshire TF3 4BX	0952–291370
Wigan	
1 Wigan Gallery, The Galleries Shopping Centre, Wigan, Greater Manchester WN1 1AR	0942–825520
Worcester	
23 Angel Place, Worcester, Hereford & Worcester WR1 3QN	0905–28010
Yeovil	
Petter House, Petters Way Yeovil, Somerset BA20 1SH	0935–75914
SCOTLAND	
Aberdeen	
The Flour Mill Lane Car Park Aberdeen, Grampian AB9 1EZ	0224–630009
Fife	
Mercat Car Park, Mercat Centre, Tolbooth St. Kirkaldy, Fife	0592–640940
Glasgow	
6th Flr. Sauchiehall Centre, 130 Sauchiehall St. Glasgow, Strathclyde G2 3ER	041–353 2594
Lothian	
King Stables Yard, King Stables Road Edinburgh, Lothian EH1 2YJ	031–225 9559
WALES	
Cardiff	
Bridge Street (bottom of multi-storey car park) Cardiff, South Glamorgan CF2 2EB	0222–399355
Cwmbran	
17 Caradoc Road (nr. MacDonalds) Town Centre, Cwmbran, Gwent	0633–362951
Newport	
193 Upper Dock St.,Newport, Gwent NP9 1DA	0633–258212/3

► USEFUL CONTACTS

British Red Cross Society (BRCS)
National Headquarters
9 Grosvenor Crescent
London SW1X 7EJ
071–235 5454

Central Region Council
(Taxicard Enquiries)
Department of Roads & Transportation
Viewforth, Stirling FK8 2ET

Community Transport Association (CTA)
Highbank
Halton Street
Hyde, Cheshire SK14 2NY
061–351 1474 or 061–366 6685

Community Transport Association Advice
and Information
061–367 8780

DIAL UK
Park Lodge, St Catherine's Hospital
Tickhill Road, Dalby
Doncaster, South Yorkshire DN4 8QN
0302–310123

Disability Action
(formerly Northern Ireland Council on
Disability)
2 Annadale Avenue
Belfast BT7 3UR
0232–491011

Edinburgh Cripple Aid Society
E.C.A.S. House
28–30 Howden Street
Edinburgh EH8 9HW
031–668 3371

National Association of Volunteer Bureaux
St Peter's College
College Road, Saltley
Birmingham B8 3TE
021–327 0265

Public Transport Information Officers
See under the appropriate county or
regional council in the main
Geographical Directory in Appendix A

The Post Office
National Post Bus Development
Road Transport Commercial Section
Burlington House, Burlington Street
Chesterfield, Derbyshire S40 1RX
0246–218317 (Chris Roberts)

The Post Office
(For post buses in England & Wales)
Public Affairs
30 St James Square
London SW1Y 4PY

The Post Office
(For post buses in Scotland)
Public Relations Unit
102 West Port
Edinburgh EH3 9HS

Passenger Transport Executives (PTEs)
See the list on Page 15 in Chapter 2
"Planning your Journey".

Royal Association for Disability and
Rehabilitation (RADAR)
25 Mortimer Street
London W1N 8AB
071–637 5400

Royal National Institute for the Blind
(RNIB)
224 Great Portland Street
London W1N 6AA
071–388 1266

St John Ambulance Association and Brigade
St John Ambulance HQ
1 Grosvenor Crescent
London SW1 7EF
071–235 5231

LOCAL TRIPS

Scottish Home and Health Department
  (SHHD)
St Andrew's House
Regent Road
Edinburgh EH1 2DE
031–556 8400

SKILL: National Bureau for Students with
  Disabilities
336 Brixton Road
London SW9 7AA
071–274 0565

**Social Services Departments (Social Work
  Departments in Scotland)**
See under the appropriate County or
  Regional Council in the main
  Geographical Directory in Appendix A.

Stroke Association
CHSA House
123–127 Whitecross Street
London EC1Y 8JJ
071–490 7999

TRIPSCOPE
63 Esmond Road
London W4 1JE
081–994 9294 (Minicom available)

AND

Pamwell House
160 Pennywell Road
Bristol BS5 0TX
0272–41904

Womens' Royal Voluntary Service (WRVS)
Headquarters
234–244 Stockwell Road
London SW9 9SP
071–416 0146

4. TRAVELLING IN AND ACROSS LONDON

TRAVELLING IN AND ACROSS LONDON

▶ CHOOSING HOW TO GO

For people with disabilities there are many ways of getting around London. It is always worth spending a little time deciding which way is the best for you.

- If you have access to a car you may wish to travel 'door-to-door', but what about traffic congestion and parking problems?

- You might still be able to travel 'door-to-door', using Dial-A-Ride, especially if you need (w) accessible transport, or transport provided by other voluntary organisations, but you will have to book ahead, and there may be restrictions on when and where they can take you.

- Private hire cars and taxis are more expensive but they can take you when and where you want to go, and more and more taxis can take you if you need to travel in your wheelchair.

- There are buses, the Underground and trains, some of which may be suitable for all or part of your journey, depending on your degree of mobility.

A combination of one or more of these may be necessary, but wherever, and whenever, you want to travel in, around or across London, there is probably a way of doing it. Finding out the *best* way for you may be more difficult, but TRIPSCOPE can help you plan a route.

There is a comprehensive guide called "Access In London", published by Nicholson and available from bookshops and RADAR. The Unit For Disabled Passengers at London Transport (LT) can help with information about travelling on public transport in London. You can also get a leaflet, "Access Around London For Disabled People", free of charge from them. If you are deaf you can obtain travel information through LT's Minicom Service.

▶ BUSES IN LONDON

If you have difficulty in walking, climbing or holding, you will find that in London, as elsewhere, modern buses are being introduced which generally have lower steps, handrails which are easier to see and grip, non-slip floors, bell-pushes which are easier to see and use. Seats near the entrance are usually reserved for elderly and disabled people, but apart from Central London, few buses have conductors who can help you get on or off.

Stationlink

'Stationlink' is a (w) accessible bus service (it can be used by everyone) which links British Rail's (BR) main London termini on a one-way circular route. It is an hourly service operated throughout the day, 7 days a week, with drivers who are specially trained to give you any help you may need. Even if you are not catching a train, the bus service itself can be a very useful, cheap way of getting around Central London.

The Airbus

If you need to get to or from London Heathrow Airport, LT runs the 'Airbus' (w) accessible bus service between Central London and all four terminals at Heathrow. There are two routes:

- A1 between Heathrow and Victoria coach and railway stations, via South Kensington;

- A2 between Heathrow and Russell Square via Bayswater, Marble Arch and Euston.

The journey lasts 50–60 minutes and the service on both routes is operated at 20–30 minute intervals throughout the day, 7 days a week. Both routes pass close to many Central London hotels and both connect with LT's 'Stationlink' service at either Victoria or Euston.

Two leaflets, "Airport/Hotel Transfer" and "Stationlink", are available free of charge from LT's Unit for Disabled Passengers.

Mobility Buses

If you need to travel in your wheelchair there are (w) accessible 'Mobility Buses' with attendants who can help you on and off the bus (the buses are for everyone, not just wheelchair users). They run on a different route each day, mainly in the suburbs, with links to local shopping centres and hospitals, but some also serve parts of Central London. A full list of routes and timetables is available from LT's Unit For Disabled Passengers.

Another (w) accessible London bus service is The Original London Sightseeing Tour (see 'Sightseeing' on page 45).

▶ THE UNDERGROUND

The Underground can be the fastest and most convenient way of travelling in and across London, but because it was built so long ago much of it is difficult for people with disabilities to use, and at peak times it can be very busy.

Stations

Access to stations usually involves at least some steps, and often long flights of stairs. Some stations have lifts (but steps have to be used as well) and many have escalators.

Trains

There is always a gap between the platform and the train, even if it is a small one. Trains have automatic or passenger operated press-button sliding doors and there are seats near the doors marked for the use of disabled and elderly people.

TRAVELLING IN AND ACROSS LONDON

Help Available

London Transport (LT) will do all it can to help you make use of the Underground, particularly if you give advance notice. Station staff will help you get to the platform and on to the train. You should contact LT's Unit For Disabled Passengers for more information. The Unit also publishes "Access To The Underground", a comprehensive guide for disabled travellers, which includes full details of access at each station. It is available by post from the Unit For Disabled Passengers, or over the counter at any LT Travel Centre.

Wheelchairs

If you use a wheelchair you can use parts of the Underground if:

- you are accompanied by someone able-bodied; AND
- you travel outside peak travelling hours; AND
- you give LT 24 hours notice.

The parts you can use are the Circle, District, East London and Metropolitan lines, and the open-air parts of other lines (but LT have plans to allow wheelchair users to travel on the underground parts of these lines as well, when they have revised their safety rules during 1993, so check with LT before you go).

If You Are Blind Or Partially Sighted

Station staff will help you to the platform if you are blind or partially sighted. Guide dogs may not travel on escalators unless they are carried, but there may be a flight of fixed stairs or a lift and outside peak times staff may be able to stop certain escalators so they can be used.

You can get a folded "Large Print" map or a "Talking Underground Map" and "Talking Underground Station Guide" cassette tape describing the Underground, free from LT's Unit For Disabled Passengers. You can get a braille map of the Underground in book form from The Royal National Institute For The Blind (RNIB). Stations and trains have public address systems but station names are not always announced by drivers.

▶ DOCKLANDS LIGHT RAILWAY

The Docklands Light Railway is a fully (w) accessible railway service between the City of London and the Docklands redevelopment area of East London. The Railway runs between Bank Station in the City, Island Gardens on the Isle of Dogs (across the Thames from Greenwich) and Stratford. It is being extended further East to Beckton.

Lifts or ramps are provided to all platforms and trains have a space for passengers in wheelchairs. Stations are unstaffed, but are monitored by closed-circuit television. Trains are automatically driven, but there is an attendant on each train to check tickets and help passengers.

During the modification to the Railway in the early 1990s to carry more passengers, parts of the service are sometimes replaced with an alternative, non (w) accessible, bus service, and lifts at some stations may not be in service, so check with LT's Travel Information Service before you go.

If You Are Blind Or Partially Sighted

A cassette tape on "Access To The Docklands Light Railway" is available from LT's Unit For Disabled Passengers.

▶ SUBURBAN RAIL SERVICES IN LONDON

British Rail (BR) staff will do all they can to help, but you should give advance notice so that the right help can be made available. This can be arranged in advance through the special 'Assistance' phone line in each local manager's office (see page 63 for details).

Access at many London suburban stations involves stairs and a bridge or subway to reach the platform. Ramps or a lift are usually available at the larger mainline stations and London terminus stations are fully (w) accessible, so it may be better to start or finish your rail journey at one of the more accessible stations, even if this involves a longer road journey to or from the station.

More modern trains have wide sliding doors, operated by push-buttons on either side of the door (people of restricted growth may have some difficulty reaching the buttons). These trains have low floors, grab rails, roomy vestibules and plenty of space for passengers in wheelchairs. Older trains have narrow doors, and if you need to travel in a wheelchair you will have to make the journey in the guard's van.

You can get more details on access at stations and to trains from your BR local manager (see page 63).

▶ TAXIS AND PRIVATE HIRE

In London all taxis (London's traditional black cabs) are licensed and have a meter which shows the fare payable. They can be hailed in the street or from a taxi rank, especially at the major railway stations, when their yellow 'for hire' sign is showing. They can also be ordered immediately by telephoning one of the taxi companies, but only a few companies take advance bookings.

Several thousand of London's taxis are (w) accessible and by the year 2000 every one of London's taxis will have to be (w) accessible by law. Already you will have little difficulty hiring a (w) accessible taxi in Central London, especially at a station, or at Heathrow Airport. These London taxi companies will accept advance bookings:

> **Black Radio Taxis**
>
> **Computer Cab Co. Ltd**
>
> **Dial-A-Cab**
>
> **Metro Radio Taxis**
>
> **Radio Taxicabs (London) Ltd**
>
> **Rainham Radio Taxis**
>
> **Taxi Trade Promotions Ltd** (for trips over 5 miles)

If you have difficulty climbing steps or holding handrails, you may find using the taxi more difficult than getting into and out of an ordinary car, but most taxi drivers will help you in or out of the cab if asked. The latest version of the 'Fairway' incorporates a swivel seat and additional step.

Private hire (or 'minicab') companies provide a car-hire service, usually with large saloon or estate cars. They are not licensed and have no meter, so you must ask what the fare will be when you book a car. The cars may *only* be booked by telephone or from a private hire office, whether you want to make an advance booking or to order one straight away. The cars are not (w) accessible but they are usually large enough for a folded wheelchair to be carried in the boot (check when you book, if necessary). You can find them advertised in the London "Yellow Pages" telephone books.

Both taxis and private hire cars may be more expensive than public transport, but they are available 24 hours a day, they can take you from door to door, which can be useful if you have heavy shopping or luggage. If there is more than one of you travelling you can share the cost.

▶ VOLUNTARY ORGANISATIONS

A number of voluntary organisations in London, as elsewhere, may be able to help with transport, whether you need to travel in a (w) accessible vehicle or can travel in an ordinary car, especially:

The British Red Cross Society (BRCS)

St. John Ambulance Association

Women's Royal Voluntary Service (WRVS)

They might be able to help with transport or escorts, especially to and from stations (although in London the WRVS can only help with escorts). TRIPSCOPE also has details of other individual operators who have transport and drivers for hire in London.

▶ DRIVING IN LONDON—PARKING

It is often difficult to find car parking space in London. If you have an Orange Badge, this will give you concessions outside the four central London boroughs at parking meters and on yellow line parking. (For full details see Chapter 6, "Cars and Driving".)

However, an Orange Badge is not generally valid for use anywhere in the City of London, the City of Westminster, the London Borough of Kensington and Chelsea, nor in the London Borough of Camden south of and including the Euston Road. This is because these parts of London have severe problems with traffic congestion and pressure on parking space. The four authorities do, however, each operate their own independent concessionary scheme for people with disabilities who live or work in the area.

It is proposed to give greater assistance to disabled people parking in Central London. Proposals under consideration include the provision of parking spaces reserved specifically for Orange Badge holders and some form of concessionary parking at meters. In addition, the London Borough of Camden is looking at the possibility of extending the Scheme to part of the area south of the Euston Road where it does not currently apply. The authorities will be working to implement these proposals at the earliest opportunity.

In the meantime, any badge holder who is planning a visit to Central London would be advised to check with the authorities what provisions are currently available in their areas and what is proposed.

Enquiries can be made to:

City of London	**071–260 1548**
Westminster	**071–222 3766**
Camden	**071–860 5979**
Kensington and Chelsea	**071–937 5464 ext.3391/2**

Nicholson's "Access In London" contains information about the location of some of the spaces reserved for disabled people as well as lots of useful information about parking in London generally.

The priority route network called 'Red Routes' is being developed in London. On a Red Route no one is allowed to stop (for waiting, parking or loading) except at designated times and in specially marked spaces, some of which will be reserved for disabled drivers. The penalties are higher than on a normal road and enforcement is stricter. The pilot Red Route is in operation and runs along the A1 from Highgate to the Angel round the ring road to Aldgate and on to the A13 Commercial Road. More routes will become operational in 1993 as the network develops. You can get further information from the Department of Transport, Room C5/19A, 2 Marsham Street, London SW1P 3EB. Telephone 071–276 6103.

Many car parks, especially at stations and shopping centres, or those operated by National Car Parks Ltd (NCP) have spaces reserved for people with disabilities (you must always display your Orange Badge when your car occupies one of these spaces).

▶ ESPECIALLY FOR VISITORS TO LONDON

Sightseeing

The London Tourist Board and Convention Centre (LTB) publishes a free leaflet, "London For All – Information For People With Disabilities", which contains a useful summary of information for disabled visitors to London.

There are sightseeing tours which can be specially arranged for individuals or groups. They are organised by people who are themselves disabled, and itineraries can be planned to meet individual needs and wishes. They are:

- **William Forrester**
- **Can Be Done**

Nicholson's "Access In London" is also a useful guide if you want to plan your own sightseeing tours.

LT operates a (w) accessible bus on its "Original London Transport Sightseeing Tour". The 1½ hour tour leaves from Wilton Road, Victoria, but it can be joined at other points in Central London as well, though you MUST telephone first. Further details and times of operation are available from LT. And don't forget that the 'Stationlink' service (see page 40 for details) can offer a cheap (w) accessible way of exploring parts of Central London by bus.

River Thames pleasure boats operate sightseeing tours from piers in Central London. Access is difficult, especially for (w) users, at the piers and on the boats, but the crews are generally helpful. You can get more information from the LTB riverboat information line.

The Visitors' Club

Membership of the Visitors' Club entitles people with disabilities to use the specially adapted and fully (w) accessible rooms of the Copthorne Tara Hotel in Central London at a substantially reduced rate. Further information on the Visitors' Club is available from the John Groom Association.

▶ ESPECIALLY FOR LONDON RESIDENTS

There are some facilities and transport schemes which are available only to disabled people who *live* in London.

Voluntary Organisations

The Greater London Association of Disabled People (GLAD) can help with transport information through their information sheets. Local community transport organisations have (w) accessible vehicles for hire to groups in the area who are members. Some run Social Car Schemes and provide other services for disabled people (eg: furniture removal) as well. The Community Transport Association (London) will have details of your local group.

A transport service may also be provided by Councils for Voluntary Service or Volunteer Bureaux, as well as those voluntary organisations already mentioned above. This is usually provided by volunteers using their own cars to give a door-to-door service for people unable to use public transport. (W) accessible transport is sometimes also available. You can find out how to contact your local Volunteer Bureau from the telephone directory or the National Association of Volunteer Bureaux.

Dial-A-Ride

Dial-A-Ride services operate throughout London with specially adapted, fully (w) accessible minibuses and helpful, specially trained drivers. You have to become a member of your local service. They provide a door-to-door service, but you do have to book in advance, usually by telephone. The services operate every day from early morning to late evening but normally only within the area of the London borough where you live. Fares are similar to those on London's buses.

You can find out more about Dial-A-Ride services in London from LT's Unit For Disabled Passengers, GLAD, or the Dial-A-Ride and Taxicard Users' Association (DART).

The London Taxicard Scheme

The London Taxicard Scheme allows disabled people who are unable to use buses or trains to travel by taxi at a cheaper rate. To join the scheme you have to be 'unable to use buses or trains by reason of blindness or any permanent or long term disability/injury which seriously impairs your ability to walk'.

You order a taxi a short while before you need it by using a special telephone number (if you need one of the (w) accessible taxis you may have to give more notice). The taxi company will send one of London's black cabs and at the end of the journey you will pay the driver (as at 1/4/92) a flat fare of £1.40 if the fare on the meter shows £10.00 or less. You may make journeys costing more than £10.00 but you will be charged the full amount over £10.00 in addition to the £1.40 flat fare.

You can make trips for any purpose you like, at any time of the day or night and take other people with you for an extra charge of 30p each.

The scheme is run on behalf of the London Borough Councils by the London Accessible Transport Unit (LATU) and application forms can be obtained from the Social Services Department of your local borough council. Some London boroughs run their own scheme (Redbridge, Barnet, the City of Westminster) and you should apply to the Social Services Department for information and an application form if you live in one of these boroughs.

▶ CONCESSIONS

Concessions are available to disabled and elderly London residents (NOT visitors) on buses, the Underground, Dockland Light Railway and BR.

You are entitled to an Elderly Person's Travel Permit if you are over 60 (women) or 65 (men). If you have a disability your local London Borough Council will consider an application from you for a Disabled Person's Travel Permit.

Your permit gives you FREE TRAVEL:

● on all Underground trains;
● on all Docklands Light Railway trains;
● on most of London Transport's ordinary bus services;
● on bus services run by other operators in London.

(You cannot use it before 9.00 a.m. on Monday to Friday, but blind permit holders under 60 or 65 can use their permit at all times.)

Permit Holders can also travel on the 'Stationlink' service for a reduced fare, but permits are not valid on the 'Airbus' service.

Your permit also gives you ½ price cheap day returns on BR trains between stations in the London area (you cannot use it before 9.30 a.m. on Monday to Friday).

You can get an application form for a permit from EITHER the Post Office OR your local borough council, depending on which borough you live in. Check with your London Borough Council Social Services Department.

Railway users who are disabled can also get a Disabled Person's Railcard, which gives substantial discounts on rail tickets. More details about these are given in Chapter 5 "Travelling Further Afield".

TRAVELLING IN AND ACROSS LONDON

Remember

- Think about the best way for you to travel in London before you go.
- It is best to avoid the early morning and early evening 'rush hour' if you can.
- If you have to travel across London alone you can get an escort to help you, or you may be able to avoid London altogether.
- The 'Stationlink' bus service is a good way of getting around Central London.
- (W) accessible services are not *just* for disabled people who *need* to travel in their wheelchair.
- More and more of London's taxis are (w) accessible and they may be cheaper than you think.

▶ GETTING ACROSS LONDON

If you do not know London, having to travel across the city to reach a port, airport or holiday destination or for a social, business or medical appointment, can be full of anxiety. However, there are some services which are especially useful if you have a disability.

Rail and Coach Terminals

If you let BR know in advance they can provide someone to help you when you arrive at the mainline terminus (see page 63 for details of the special telephone numbers in BR Local Managers' Offices). Help can also be made available at Victoria Coach Station, if they are told by you or your booking agent at least 5 days in advance what coach you will be arriving on, or need to catch.

Taxis and Private Hire

For someone unfamiliar with London a taxi may be the easiest way of travelling from station to station. You should have no difficulty in getting a (w) accessible taxi at station taxi ranks, without having to book in advance.

Stationlink

The 'Stationlink' (w) accessible bus service can be used by everyone and links BR's main London termini. It may be the best way of getting across Central London. The service is explained in the section on BUSES on page 40.

The Airbus

If you need to get to or from London Heathrow Airport, LT runs the 'Airbus' (w) accessible bus service between Central London and all four terminals at Heathrow. There are two routes between the Airport and Central London which pass close to many Central London hotels and both connect with LT's 'Stationlink' service at either Victoria or Euston. The service is described more fully under BUSES on page 41.

The Gatwick and Stansted Expresses

BR operates the (w) accessible Gatwick Express from London's Victoria station non-stop to Gatwick Airport every 15 minutes throughout the day, every day. The journey takes 30 minutes. A similar service, The Stansted Express, links London Liverpool Street and Stansted Airport Station.

Thameslink

If you are travelling from the north of London to the south (or vice versa), it may be more convenient to use BR's (w) accessible Thameslink service which runs between Bedford and Brighton via Luton, St. Albans, Central London and Gatwick. The only (w) accessible Central London stations on this route are City Thameslink and London Bridge, but it is one way to cross London without having to change trains. There are also some InterCity rail services between the north of England and the south which avoid London altogether.

Voluntary Organisations

The voluntary organisations already mentioned in this chapter (on page 44) may be able to help you across London, especially between stations, by providing an escort.

▶ USEFUL CONTACTS

British Red Cross Society (BRCS)
(London)
106 Crawford Street
London W1H 1AL
071–935 4981

Can Be Done
7–11 Kensington High Street
London W8 5NP
081–907 2400

Dial-A-Ride & Taxicard Users' Association
 (DART)
St. Margarets
25 Leighton Road
London NW5 2QD
071–482 2325

London Accessible Transport Unit
(Taxicard Section)
Britannia House
1–11 Glenthorne Road
London W6 OLF
081–748 7272

Greater London Association of Disabled
 People (GLAD)
336 Brixton Road
London SW9 7AA
071–274 0107

John Groom Association
10 Gloucester Drive
London N4 2LP
081–802 7272

Community Transport Association (London)
The Arlington Road Works Depot, A Block
211 Arlington Road
London NW1 7HD
071–911 0959

London Transport
  Unit For Disabled Passengers
  55 Broadway
  London SW1H 0BD
  071–222 5600

  Travel Information Service
  071–222 1234

  (Minicom 071–918 3015)

London Tourist Board and Convention
 Bureau
26 Grosvenor Gardens
London SW1W ODU

  Tourist Information: 071–730 3488
  Riverboat Information: 071–730 4812

TRAVELLING IN AND ACROSS LONDON

National Association of Volunteer Bureaux
St Peter's College
College Road
Saltley, Birmingham B8 3TE
021–327 0265

Orange Badge enquiries (parking):

General:

Department of Transport
Room C10/02
2 Marsham Street
London SW1P 3EB
071–276 6291

Central London:

City of London Corporation
Public Relations Department
P O Box 270, The Guildhall
London EC2P 2EJ
071–260 1548

Westminster:

Disabled Parking Exemption Officer
Capital Parking Ltd
PO Box 601
London SW1H 9BS
071–222 3766

Camden:

Phoenix Court
Brill Place
London NW1 1HB
071–860 5979

Kensington & Chelsea:

Highways & Traffic Section
Town Hall
Hornton Street
London W8 7NX
071–937 5464 Ext.3391/2

Royal Association for Disability and
   Rehabilitation (RADAR)
25 Mortimer Street
London W1N 8AB
071–637 5400

Royal National Institute for the Blind
   (RNIB)
224 Great Portland Street
London W1N 6AA
071–388 1266

St John Ambulance Association and Brigade
   (for London)
Prince of Wales District
Edwina Mountbatten House
63 York Street
London W1H 1PS
071–258 3456 (Ext. 139 for transport)

Taxi Companies (Advance Booking)

Black Radio Taxis
081–209 0211

Computer Cab Co Ltd
071–286 0666

Dial-A-Cab
071–253 5000

Metro Radio Taxis
071–538 0033

Radio Taxicabs (London) Ltd
071–272 0272

Rainham Radio Taxis
081–592 1019

Taxi Trade Promotions Ltd
071–700 5681

Department of Transport
(For information on 'Red Routes')
Room C5/19A
2 Marsham Street
London SW1P 3EB
071–276 6103

TRIPSCOPE
63 Esmond Road
London W4 1JE
081–994 9294 (Minicom available)

AND

Pamwell House
160 Pennywell Road
Bristol BS5 0TX
0272–414094

Victoria Coach Station
164 Buckingham Palace Road
London SW1W 9TP
071–730 0202 (General Information &
   Assistance)

William Forrester
1 Belvedere Close
Guildford, Surrey GU2 6NP
0483–575401

Women's Royal Voluntary Service (WRVS)
234–244 Stockwell Road
London SW9 9SP
071–416 0146
(ask for: Family Welfare Dept. for escorts in
   London)

5. TRAVELLING FURTHER AFIELD

CONTENTS   PAGE NO.

▶ CHOOSING HOW TO GO

Travelling longer distances in Britain usually means going by train, coach or plane, unless you have a car, or there is someone who can take you door-to-door.

TRAVELLING FURTHER AFIELD

Travelling in your own car is a relatively easy and cheap way of travelling long distance. There are no changes and you can choose your own time of travel. (There is more about cars and driving in Chapter 6.) If you do not have access to a car, travelling long distance can be very expensive if you want to go door-to-door. If you use the transport provided by commercial operators, and even voluntary organisations, there is generally a mileage charge which also covers the 'empty' return journey for the driver.

Travelling by train is now a lot more comfortable on InterCity services, but you will have to get from home to the station, and from the station to your final destination at the other end of the journey. Going by coach will usually be the cheapest way of all (although there are no concessionary fares for people with disabilities), but nearly all coaches on scheduled services have high entrance steps and are not accessible if you have to travel in your wheelchair. Again, you have to think about getting to and from the coach stations; but there are probably more direct cross-country coach services than long distance rail services. Domestic flights can be the fastest way of travelling, but they are probably the most expensive, and you have to get to and from the airports. It may only be worthwhile going by air in the UK if you have to travel very long distances, and your journey to and from the airport is not very far.

TRIPSCOPE will be happy to help you choose the means of travel which best suits you, and to let you know about what concessions may be available.

▶ LONG-DISTANCE RAIL TRAVEL

Planning Your Journey

Local, or suburban, rail travel is covered in Chapter 3, and Chapter 4 has a section on travel (including rail) in and across London. Chapter 6 deals with rail travel in Europe. If you are travelling by local train to connect with a mainline or InterCity service you should read these sections as well.

If you need help British Rail (BR) will do all it can to give it, but would like its staff to be given advance notice so that the necessary arrangements can be made. Two days is ideal, but even a few hours' notice can make all the difference.

If you are severely disabled and need special arrangements or assistance from BR staff you should make contact in advance with your local manager. The appropriate phone number can be found in the leaflet "British Rail and Disabled Travellers", available from principal stations, Travel Centres and travel agents, and phone numbers are also given in the panel on page 63. If you make arrangements some time in advance, it is worth checking the **day before you travel** that the arrangements have been made and you are expected.

Whatever your disability, you may find it easier to make a longer journey by road to a mainline station where facilities tend to be better, or to avoid having to change trains. You need to bear this in mind too where stations are unstaffed all the time and there will be no one there to help you.

> **NOTE:** Some stations are staffed only part of the time so you should check beforehand with your local manager whether there will be help available at the station when you want to travel (and when you want to return!).

Wherever you are on BR, signs with a **purple background** show where there are special facilities to help people with disabilities.

People with Wheelchairs and Walking Difficulties

Parking

There is often short-stay parking close to station entrances. Some spaces may be marked for use by disabled people, and sometimes special arrangements can be made for parking close to a suitable entrance when BR staff know in advance of your travel plans. Some stations have special car parking spaces for people with disabilities, although in London and some other large cities these may be limited. In some areas where it is difficult to park near a station there may be Park-and-Ride facilities. For more information you should contact your BR local manager.

Stations

Most platforms at mainline stations can be reached by ramps or lifts, but sometimes it may be necessary for staff to take you by an alternative route.

Improvements to stations are being made in many places. Disabled persons' toilets, many of them unisex, are being installed at principal stations. These toilets are clearly signed with the international disabled symbol and are fitted with National Key Scheme (NKS) locks. The Royal Association for Disability and Rehabilitation (RADAR) can supply keys under this scheme. If you do not have your own key, some station toilets have notices saying where a key can be obtained. The toilets are usually kept locked to deter vandalism.

In many parts of the country 'Open Stations' are being introduced. Here, ticket barriers have been abolished and all ticket checks are carried out on trains (ask for a leaflet from any principal station or TravelCentre). You should allow yourself enough time to get a ticket **before starting your journey**, as a passenger boarding a train without a ticket is liable to pay the full Standard single or return fare. At stations with ticket barriers people meeting or seeing off disabled or blind passengers do not need a platform ticket.

Many mainline stations have portable ramps and wheelchairs to help people with walking difficulties get on and off trains. At principal stations, wheelchairs are available to take you from the station entrance to the booking office and/or your train.

RADAR has produced a guide in cooperation with BR, entitled "A Guide to British Rail for Disabled People", available from RADAR. This gives information on access to over 500 principal stations.

Facilities on Trains

CROSS-COUNTRY TRAINS have been improved and now have wide sliding doors, operated by push-buttons. People of restricted growth may, however, have some difficulty reaching these buttons. These trains have low floors, grabrails and space for passengers in wheelchairs. There is no accommodation on these trains for large 'runabout' vehicles.

INTERCITY trains mostly now have wide doors and handy grabrails, and if you need to travel in your wheelchair you should be able to travel within the passenger accommodation. Modern coaches also have automatic interior doors to make it easier to walk through the train.

In the latest trains, including InterCity 125 and 225 High Speed trains, there is at least one coach in Standard Class which has space to enable you to travel in your own wheelchair (provided it doesn't exceed the maximum width of 67 cms. or 26½ inches). You need to make a reservation in advance to be sure it is available on the train of your choice. If you have restricted leg movement or another disability, the gangway seat opposite the wheelchair space on most InterCity trains can be specially reserved. This seat is close to the doorway and the toilet. You can always ask to reserve seats closest to the doorways.

The Gatwick Express (running between London-Victoria and Gatwick Airport) and the Stansted Express (running between London-Liverpool Street and Stansted Airport) are both fully (w) accessible and no advance notice is necessary.

All scheduled InterCity services, and the cross country services run by Regional Railways, now use modern trains which have one or more (w) accessible coaches. However, there may still be an occasion when unforeseen circumstances lead to a train with older coaches having to be used. On such an occasion, if you are unable to transfer from your wheelchair to an ordinary seat, you will have to travel in the guard's van (but a discount on the fare may be available; see the section on "Concessions" on page 61).

TOILETS adapted for wheelchair users are being introduced on trains on many long-distance routes. You should ask about this facility when you book your ticket. Toilets on other trains are not at present accessible to people who cannot walk.

You may wish to consider making advance arrangements to break your journey at a station with (w) accessible toilet facilities and resume your journey by the next suitable train, though this process could be somewhat of an added burden, with an inevitable delay.

Alternatively there are discreet self-help measures you can take. The Disabled Living Foundation (DLF) and Disability Scotland can supply details.

REFRESHMENTS are available on trains with a restaurant car, buffet or trolley service. On many trains full meals are served to passengers in First Class seats. Drinks and light refreshments can be brought to your seat in either First or Standard Class.

INTERCITY SLEEPERS now all use air-conditioned carriages. Compartments are convertible for twin or single berth use and communicating doors between pairs of compartments allow you to be close to your travelling companion if you are severely disabled. An attendant is on duty throughout the journey and can be called by a bell-push next to each berth. *Because of the confined space which makes transfer from a wheelchair to a berth difficult, travel by sleeper is not recommended if you have to travel in your wheelchair.*

Help for Blind and Partially Sighted People

Stations

BR staff will help guide you, although it is better to arrange this in advance. On platforms used by high-speed trains there is a yellow line 1.5 metres from the edge. You should stand behind this for safety.

At principal stations details of all departing trains are given by public announcement and details of trains arriving may also be announced.

Trains

On most InterCity trains door handles are only on the outside of the coach and are reached by lowering the window. InterCity 225 trains used on the East Coast route have wide sliding doors, operated by push-buttons. On most InterCity trains internal doors open automatically and announcements are made about approaching station stops, services and catering.

Guide Dogs

Guide dogs travel free with blind people. They may be taken into buffets and restaurants at stations and on trains. Staff will ensure that both traveller and dog are seated in the most convenient location in the dining area.

Your guide dog may travel with you in a sleeping compartment if you book in advance. You will travel in a single-berth compartment for only one Standard Class fare and berth fee. You should take a rug or blanket for your dog to sleep on.

Help for People with Hearing or Speech Impairments

Stations

Many principal stations have large electronic indicators or computer-controlled TV screens to display up-to-the-minute information on train departures and arrivals, as well as the usual printed timetables.

Mainline stations have public telephones which are fitted with an inductive coupler. It can be used in the usual way with any hearing aid fitted with a 'T' switch. These telephones are marked with the international 'ear' symbol of people who are deaf or hard of hearing. Travel Centre staff will provide written information, but it helps to have a notepad handy for the journey. The Royal National Institute for Deaf People (RNID) produces small 'Helping Hand' pads of forms which you can use to write out your ticket and train-time request to hand to station staff. (You can get these from the RNID or at most stations.) As stations are modernised, ticket offices are being fitted with induction loops. You will be able to identify which ones have been fitted by the the distinctive sticker.

Trains

Many InterCity and cross-country trains show their destinations on, or adjacent to, the carriage doors. A notepad is even more important for on-the-train information.

Motorail

Motorail services operate between:

London (Euston) and	—	Carlisle, Edinburgh, Fort William, Aberdeen and Inverness;
Bristol and	—	Edinburgh

Specialist staff will drive your car on and off the train. Wheelchairs are available if you need help from your car to the train. Sleeping cars are used on overnight services and, as mentioned earlier in this Chapter, travel by sleeper is not recommended if you have to travel in your wheelchair. On day services standard InterCity coaches are used, so if you need to travel in your wheelchair you should be able to travel within the passenger accommodation. For full details you can get a free "Motorail" leaflet at principal stations, Travel Centres and from travel agents.

Getting Across London

See the panel on page 48 for details on how to get from one London rail terminus to another, and on how to use rail services to avoid changing trains in London altogether.

Travelling by Rail in Northern Ireland

If you are going to Northern Ireland you may find the following information on rail travel useful.

The railway in Northern Ireland is operated by Northern Ireland Railways Company Ltd., a private company. If you have a disability and will need assistance, you are advised to give advance notice of any intended journey so that the right help can be given.

Stations

All stations except Carrickfergus are (w) accessible but only Belfast Central and Larne Harbour Stations have good internal accessibility. The few stations with (w) accessible toilets are Belfast Central, Larne Harbour and Portadown.

Trains

Castle Class trains are equipped with wide, automatic doors and folding seats to provide ease of access and additional wheelchair space. Cross-border services have space available to accommodate wheelchairs.

Useful Contacts

For information on all of the above you should contact:

Northern Ireland Railways Company Ltd
Central Station
East Bridge Street
Belfast BT1 3PB
0232–230310 (Information)
0232–235282 (Administration)

▶ **COACH TRAVEL**

Coach Stations

Some coach stations, usually the more modern ones, are well designed for people with disabilities, with ramps, level access and (w) accessible toilets and buffets. In other, older stations you may find it difficult getting into the station, the toilets, or the refreshment areas if you are in a wheelchair or have difficulty in walking and climbing.

At London's Victoria Coach Station hostesses are available to help if you need assistance with getting on and off coaches and with changing services. You should check with your booking agent at least 5 days before travelling, so that the necessary arrangements can be made.

Local Access Guides may give details of facilities, or you can ask your local coach travel office to find out for you and to arrange whatever help you need at both ends of your journey and any intermediate stops.

Coaches

Coaches usually have more and higher steps than buses, and those on scheduled services are not (w) accessible.

Some companies do have coaches fitted with a lift so that passengers can travel in wheelchairs. These coaches are usually for hire to groups. It is worth checking with your local coach operator, or you can contact the Bus and Coach Council for further information.

If you can travel in a coach seat, coach station staff may be able to help you on board and will stow your wheelchair in the luggage compartment at no extra cost. National Express require 7 days' notice for this, so you should request this help when you make your booking.

Nowadays more coaches have toilets on board but these are not fully accessible. Alternatively, stops are often made at intermediate coach stations or motorway service areas.

▶ DOMESTIC FLIGHTS

The information you will need to assist you with air travel is generally applicable to both international and domestic flights, and you should read the section on International Air Travel in Chapter 7 "Travelling Abroad". However, there are special concessions (see page 62) which can be applicable for blind and partially sighted people on domestic flights only.

▶ DOOR-TO-DOOR TRANSPORT

If you have no transport of your own and you have a mobility handicap which prevents you using public transport, some voluntary organisations may be able to help with longer distance trips, although many have been set up to provide specifically local transport for people with disabilities. These door-to-door transport services are usually operated by helpful, specially trained staff.

The schemes vary from those operated with ordinary cars to those run with (w) adapted minibuses. You usually have to book in advance and make a payment based on the mileage, or give a donation. For longer distance journeys it may be better, and usually cheaper, to use a local voluntary transport scheme to take you to a bus, coach or railway station to link up with the coach or rail services.

If the availability of toilets for disabled people is a worry, on longer trips, don't forget the National Key Scheme. RADAR can supply keys and details of the location of these fully (w) accessible toilets under this scheme.

Community Transport

Local Community Transport (CT) organisations usually have a pool of vehicles which they will hire out to local member groups or associations, with or without a driver (depending on the particular CT group). If your own group wants to hire a vehicle and supply its own driver, the driver will usually be required to meet certain conditions and also to take a familiarisation test.

The vehicles are generally, but not always, (w) accessible and can be hired by most local community groups including disability organisations. Some CT organisations run Social Car Schemes and provide other services for disabled people (eg: furniture removal) as well. To find out whether there is a CT organisation in your area you should contact the Community Transport Association. The Department of Transport (DoT) can supply a "Directory of Voluntary and Community Transport", covering either the whole country or on a county-by-county basis. It is available free of charge from the Disability Unit at the DoT.

Dial-a-Ride

Most services will only take you on trips in the local area where they are based but a few might be prepared to go further afield. More information about Dial-a-Ride services can be found on page 23 in Chapter 3 "Local Trips".)

Social Car Schemes

Some organisations run Social Car Schemes with volunteer drivers. The volunteers use their own cars to drive people who cannot use public transport, mainly on local trips, but some will travel longer distances. There is a charge, based on the mileage involved (remember it will include the empty return journey for the driver as well). Some schemes will take you anywhere you want to go but others will only take you on local trips to hospital appointments, to doctors' surgeries, or to collect prescriptions.

The schemes are run by a variety of organisations:

● *Local Volunteer Bureaux or local Voluntary Services Councils* (although NOT ALL run transport schemes). Check with your local transport guide if your county council publishes one (see the panel on page 28), or with your local Citizens Advice Bureau for further information;

● *Local Authority Social Services Departments (Social Work Departments in Scotland).* A very few run Social Car Schemes with volunteer drivers;

● *CT Organisations.* Some run a Social Car Scheme;

● *Women's Royal Voluntary Service (WRVS).* Mainly for health or welfare purposes (they do not supply transport in the London area) and sometimes the Social Car Scheme is run by them for the county council; and

● *The British Red Cross Society (BRCS)*

If you need (w) accessible transport this can be provided with the ambulances of the BRCS or St John Ambulance Society but the cost of the journey will be higher than that for travelling in an ordinary car.

Other Voluntary Organisations

Many disability groups and other organisations such as Age Concern, Multiple Sclerosis Society branches, and PHAB clubs have (w) accessible minibuses for taking their own members on outings, to social events etc. Usually they are for the exclusive use of their own members, but some groups do make their vehicles available to other organisations, or will take you as a passenger, with their own driver. You should check with the individual local group to find out whether such hiring is possible.

Escorts

If you are travelling alone and need someone to go with you, escorts can be provided by WRVS and BRCS. Of course, their fares to and from home and expenses (meals if it is a long journey) will have to be paid. BRCS supplies trained escorts, but WRVS escorts are not medically qualified and cannot offer nursing care on the journey.

▶ FERRIES—UK ESTUARIES AND ISLANDS

Many of the smaller ferries, such as those linking the mainland with the Scottish Islands, do not have good facilities for people with disabilities.

Shorter crossings are often operated with open-deck ferries on which you can stay in your vehicle, but on longer crossings with enclosed car-decks this may not be possible. The majority of these ferries are of a smaller and older type without lifts, ramps, or toilets adapted for wheelchair users.

If you need help, you should contact the ferry company in advance to make the necessary arrangements. Many of the ferry companies do give discounts on the cost of the ferry crossing to disabled motorists (see "Concessions" below).

The panel on page 65 gives brief details on the main UK domestic ferry crossings. For more information about cross-Channel ferries you should see this section of Chapter 7 "Travelling Abroad".

▶ CONCESSIONS

British Rail

Disabled Persons Railcard

This is available to permanently and severely disabled people and includes people who are blind or partially sighted, deaf with or without speech, and those with a liability to recurrent attacks of epilepsy. A Railcard entitles the holder (and a companion, if you wish) to a reduction of between a half and one-third off the price of a range of BR tickets. It costs £14 and is valid for a year. To find out if you qualify, you can get a leaflet, "Disabled Persons Railcard", including an application form, from BR stations, Travel Centres and main Post Offices.

Wheelchair Users

If you do not hold a Railcard and you need to travel in your own wheelchair, you can still get discounts of a half to one-third off the price of Single, Open Return and Day Return fares (first or standard class) and the same discounts apply to one companion travelling with you. You will have to hold a Disabled Persons Railcard to get a discount on any cheaper types of ticket when these are available.

Powered and unpowered wheelchairs can be taken with you on trains free of charge. Large 'runabout' vehicles can ONLY be carried when guards' van space is available and there will be a charge for taking them. (Be sure to ask about this early on in planning your journey.)

If you need to travel in your wheelchair it may be necessary for you to travel in the guard's van on some trains. If you are a Disabled Persons Railcard holder and you are making a longer distance journey with an Open Return, Network Awaybreak or Saver ticket you can claim a refund of half the fare for that part of the journey travelled in the guard's van. You must ask the guard to endorse the back of your ticket and then apply to the booking office for the refund.

Blind and Partially Sighted People

Guide dogs accompanying blind people are always carried free of charge. If you are registered blind or partially sighted, travelling *with* a companion, discounts of a half to one-third are available for both of you on Single, Open Return, Day Return and Season tickets. You must hold a Disabled Persons Railcard to get a discount on any cheaper types of ticket when available.

Concessions are also available for registered blind people travelling with a companion to a number of continental countries (see page 92, Chapter 7 "Travelling Abroad"). More details are available from stations which issue tickets for rail travel to Europe.

Coaches

Whilst there are generally no concessions on coach fares for people with disabilities, some companies do offer fare concessions for elderly people.

Air Travel

Blind and Partially Sighted People

There are concessions for blind passengers travelling for business, medical, training or rehabilitation purposes on UK domestic flights (including to and from the Channel Islands, Isle of Man and Eire). If this applies to you, you and an escort can travel toether for one adult fare. In the same circumstances your guide dog can invariably travel free of charge with you in the cabin of the aircraft. Remember that if you intend to take your guide dog abroad, the normal 6 month quarantine period also applies to guide dogs on return to the UK! You should contact the Guide Dogs for the Blind Association first, to discuss the implications this raises for care of your dog on the flight and while abroad, and for arrangements while in quarantine on your return to the UK.

Ferries

Most ferry companies offer substantial discounts (50% or 100%) on the car fare for members of one of the recognised disabled motoring organisations (for more information about these see Chapter 6 "Cars and Driving"). If you are not a member of one of these organisations you may still be able to get a concession by obtaining a form from the ferry company signed by your local Social Services Department.

Remember

- Door-to-door travel is expensive for longer trips if you do not have your own car.

- Give as much notice as you can when travelling by public transport, so that the right arrangements can be made for the help you need AND

- double-check the day before you go that everything is ready for you.

- Facilities and assistance available when travelling by train are improving.

- Rail fares can be cheaper with a Disabled Persons Railcard, but there are concessions ANYWAY if you travel in a wheelchair or you are blind or partially sighted.

- Coaches on scheduled services are not (w) accessible, but they are a cheap way of making long-distance journeys if you can manage the steps.

- If you are using domestic air services, there is more information on flying in Chapter 7 "Travelling Abroad".

▶ **BRITISH RAIL LOCAL MANAGERS' OFFICES**—*Contact Telephone Numbers*

Ashford
0233–617299

Bath Spa
0272–347570

Birmingham New Street
021–644 4288

Brighton
0273–24469/24487

Bristol Temple Meads
0272–348612

Cambridge
0223–453985

Carlisle
0228–515439

Chester
0244–346737

Crewe
0270–532727

Derby
0332–264829

Ealing Broadway
081–813 5070

East Midlands
(Derby, Leicester, Nottingham)
0332–386925

Exeter
0392–72281

Gatwick Airport
0293–524167

Leeds
0532–411725

Leicester
0332–264829

Liverpool
051–709 8292 ext.2707

London Bridge
071–922 4548

London Euston
071–922 6482

London King's Cross
071–922 9091

London Liverpool Street
071–928 5151 ext.52789/90

London Marylebone
071–922 9522

TRAVELLING FURTHER AFIELD

London Paddington
071–922 6742

London St. Pancras
071–922 6466

London Victoria
071–922 6215

London Waterloo
071–922 4500

Manchester
061–228 4342

Newcastle
091–261 1234 ext.2617

Norwich
0603–285664

Nottingham
0602–418531 ext.2592

Oxford
0865–722333

Penzance
0736 64830

Peterborough
0733–346603

Plymouth
0752–221300

Preston
0772–54821 ext.2246 (InterCity)
or 2513 (Regional Railways)

Reading
0734–579334

Sheffield
0742–720002 ext.2210

Shrewsbury
0743–241971

Slough
0753–537343

Southampton
0703–728059

Southend
0702–354413

Swindon
0793–526100

Taunton
0823–283444

Truro
0872–76244

Watford
0923–56430

York
0904–523739

SCOTLAND

Aberdeen
0224–210210

Ayr
0292–267135 ext.8526/8557

Dundee
0382–305263

Edinburgh
031–556 2477 ext.2461

Fort William
0397–703791

Glasgow Central
041–335 4352

Inverness
0463–245132

Perth
0738–46233

Scotrail North West
041–335 7573

WALES

Cardiff
0222–499811
ext. 2713 (InterCity)
      2554 (Regional Railways)

Mid Wales
0743–241971

North Wales
0244–346737

Swansea
0792–632286

▶ **MAIN UK FERRY ROUTES**

SERVICE	FERRY COMPANY AND SPECIAL FACILITIES
Between the Orkney Is.	*Orkney Islands Shipping Co.*
Scrabster—Stromness **Stromness—Lerwick** **Aberdeen—Lerwick** **Aberdeen—Orkney Is.**	*P & O Scottish Ferries Ltd.* Overnight ferries have cabins designed to suit the needs of disabled people.
Portsmouth—Fishbourne, IOW **Lymington—Yarmouth, IOW**	*Wight Link Ltd* BR Disabled Persons' Railcard holders get one third off the fare and an accompanying passenger travels free.
Southampton—Cowes	*Red Funnel Ferries.* Check first as one of three vessels on this route is not suitable for disabled passengers, but the other two have good (w) access and a (w) accessible toilet.
Poole—Jersey/Guernsey	*British Channel Island Ferries*, due in 1992, 'MV Beuport', has good access throughout with adapted cabins and (w) accessible toilets.
Weymouth—Channel Is.	*Condor Ltd.* operates catamaran hydrofoil services to and between the Channel Islands. Will give assistance with advance notice.
Fleetwood—Douglas (Summer only) **Heysham—Douglas**	*Isle Of Man Steam Packet Co.* Lift from car to passenger deck but no (w) accessible toilets.
Stranraer—Larne	*Sealink Stena Line.* Most ships have facilities for disabled passengers and assistance given with advance notice.
Cairnryan—Larne	*P & O European Ferries Ltd.* All ships are (w) accessible with lifts and (w) accessible toilets.
Islay—Jura—Gourock **Dunoon**	*Harrison Clyde Ltd.*
The Clyde—Oban—Mull **Islay—Skye—Western** **Isles—Outer Isles**	*Caledonian MacBrayne Ltd.* Access on some vessels not easy but newest ones are fully (w) accessible with lifts.

TRAVELLING FURTHER AFIELD

▶ USEFUL CONTACTS

British Rail (BR)—see the list of BR Local
Managers' Offices (panel on page 63)

British Red Cross Society (BRCS)
National Headquarters
9 Grosvenor Crescent
London SW1X 7EJ
071–235 5454

Bus and Coach Council
Sardinia House
52 Lincoln's Inn Fields
London WC2A 3LZ
071–831 7546

Community Transport Association (CTA)
Highbank
Halton Street
Hyde, Cheshire SK14 2NY
061–351 1474 Or 061–366 6685

Community Transport Association Advice &
Information
061–367 8780

Disability Unit
Department of Transport
Room S10/21
2 Marsham Street
London SW1P 3EB
071–276-5257 (Minicom 071–276 4973)

Disability Scotland
Princes House
5 Shandwick Place
Edinburgh EH2 4RG
031–229 8632

Disabled Living Foundation (DLF)
380–384 Harrow Road
London W9 2HU
071–289 6111

Ferry Companies (Domestic Routes)

British Channel Island Ferries
Passenger Ferry Terminal
New Harbour Road
Poole, Dorset BH15 4AJ
0202–681155

Caledonian MacBrayne Ltd
Ferry Terminal
Gourock, Strathclyde PA19 1QP
0475–33755

Condor Weymouth Ltd
Weymouth Quay
Weymouth, Dorset DT4 8DX
0305–761551

Harrison Clyde Ltd
16 Woodside Crescent
Glasgow G3 7UT
041–332 9766

Isle Of Man Steam Packet Co.
PO Box 5
Imperial Buildings
Douglas, Isle Of Man
0624–661661

AND

Sea Terminal
Heysham, Lancs. LA3 2XF
0524–853802

Orkney Islands Shipping Co.
4 Ayre Road
Kirkwall, Orkney Islands
0856–2044

P & O European Ferries Ltd
Cairnryan, nr. Stranraer
Wigtown DG9 8BR
0581–2276

P & O Scottish Ferries Ltd
PO Box 5
Jamiesons Quay
Aberdeen AB9 8DL
0224–589111

Red Funnel Ferries
12 Bugle Street
Southampton, Hants. SO9 4LT
0703–330333

Sealink Stena Line
Charter House
Park Street
Ashford, Kent TN24 8EX
0233–647022

AND

Larne
Co. Antrim
0574–273616

Wight Link Ltd
Gun Wharf Road
Portsmouth, Hants. PO1 2LA
0705–812911

Guide Dogs for the Blind Association
Hillfields, Burghfield Common
Reading, Berks. RG7 3YG
0734–835555

National Association of Volunteer Bureaux
St. Peter's College
College Road
Saltley, Birmingham B8 3TE
021–327 0265

Royal Association for Disability and
 Rehabilitation (RADAR)
25 Mortimer Street
London WC1N 8AB
071–637 5400

Royal National Institute for Deaf People
 (RNID)
105 Gower Street
London WC1E 6AH
071–387 8033

TRIPSCOPE
63 Esmond Road
London W4 1JE
081–994 9294 (Minicom available)

AND

Pamwell House
160 Pennywell Road
Bristol BS5 OTX
0272–414094

Victoria Coach Station
164 Buckingham Palace Road
London SW1W 9TP
071–730 0202

Women's Royal Voluntary Service (WRVS)
Headquarters
234–244 Stockwell Road
London SW9 9SP
071–416 0146

6. CARS AND DRIVING

CARS AND DRIVING

▶ **CARS**

Help with Buying a Car

Affording a car

There are several ways to get help to buy a car, whether to drive yourself or for someone to drive for you. Some options are more attractive at first sight than others, but it is well worth exploring them all. A useful reference for most aspects of car ownership is "Motoring and Mobility for Disabled People", available from the Royal Association for Disability and Rehabilitation (RADAR). The Mobility Advice and Vehicle Information Service (MAVIS) also gives advice, either by telephone or letter, or you can contact one of the other Assessment Centres listed on page 81.

New or secondhand cars

There are two organisations which are able to help you to buy a new car: Motability and Aid Vehicle Supplies (AVS). Both Motability and AVS have schemes for purchasing secondhand cars.

If you are thinking of buying secondhand through Motability, the AA will vet prospective purchases for a moderate fee; and reputable dealers operate the Motor Agents' Association warranty for cars under 6 years old.

For new cars, some manufacturers offer discounts to registered disabled people in the range of 10% to 17%. These do not usually apply if you want to part-exchange a car, and some depend on the individual dealer. "Discounts and Concessions Fact Sheet No. 9", available from RADAR, gives full details of discounts currently available, or you can get advice from one of the disabled motoring organisations:

● The Disabled Drivers' Association (DDA)
● The Disabled Drivers' Motor Club (DDMC)
● The Disabled Motorists' Federation (DMF).

Invalid Vehicles ('Trikes')

Will continue to be maintained so long as serviceable replacements and parts are available. They are no longer issued to new applicants. You can, if you wish, switch to the 'Mobility Component' of the Disability Living Allowance (DLA) and use that to buy an ordinary car. It may be possible that Motability will help pay for your driving lessons (if you're a trike driver) and also offer financial help with adaptations. For further details you should contact Motability.

You can keep the trike for 6 months while you obtain a car and learn to drive it. If you are unable to cope with driving a car, or fail the driving test, you can hand the car back and retain your trike.

Motability

This scheme allows the use of the Mobility Component of your DLA (as with the old Mobility Allowance) or War Pensioners' Mobility Supplement for hiring or purchasing a new car on hire purchase. These allowances can also be used for purchasing a new wheelchair, electric scooter or a secondhand car on hire purchase. Anyone who receives one of the above allowances can hire or purchase a car. You do not have to be a driver. A car may be hired or purchased with DLA (Mobility Component) on behalf of a child passenger.

Contract Hire with Motability (previously known as Leasing)

This hire scheme means that you give over your DLA (Mobility Component) or Supplement and future increases to Motability for the next 3 years, in return for which you rent a car.

Points to bear in mind:

- You have to pay any extra rental required over and above your allowance, in a lump sum as an advance payment. An approximate average would be £2,000. However, this can range from nothing for some models (such as a Fiesta, Mini or Nova) to £8,000 for a top-of-the-range Volvo.

- Depending on the make of car you hire you may be required to pay a delivery charge somewhere in the region of £300. However, this mainly applies to those living in Northern Ireland and some parts of Scotland. You should check with your car dealer to find out if this applies to your car.

- All maintenance and service costs over the 3-year period are included, but it will be your responsibility to get the car to and from your dealer for regular servicing and, if required, to have the car promptly repaired. Failure to comply with this requirement would break your hire contract!

- If your mileage exceeds an average of 12,000 miles a year, you will have to pay an additional amount related to the excess each year.

- Motability Insurance is a fleet/block policy and is fully comprehensive at no additional cost, but this policy does not cover the use of vehicles for business purposes. Also, this type of insurance does not allow for 'no claims' bonuses.

- The cost of any adaptations (eg: hand controls, etc.), and their removal after 3 years, will be an additional expense for you. If any major adaptations, such as joy stick or foot steering, are necessary it is possible that you would be better off purchasing a car through the Motability Hire Purchase scheme.

- If you cannot afford the advance payment or the extra cost of adaptations, you may be eligible for help from Motability's Special Charitable Fund.

  NOTE: This fund is very limited. Therefore you must ensure that you've chosen the cheapest car suitable for your needs. **No assistance will be given to meet the running costs of your car.**

CARS AND DRIVING

● From April 1991, £1 million a year (for 3 years) has been made available by the Government to help severely disabled people needing expensive adaptations and controls. This help is available for people using the contract hire or hire purchase schemes.

Hire purchase using Motability

New cars: The hire purchase scheme means that you surrender all or part of your DLA (Mobility Component) or Supplement for a fixed rate for the term of contract, which will be 4, 4½ or 5 years.

Second hand cars: The same applies to hire purchase of second hand cars but the term of contract will be 2 or 3 years. When purchasing a second hand car it must be under 4 years old and have done less than 40,000 miles. In some cases the car must be under 3 years old and have done less than 30,000 miles, e.g. Hyundai, Lada, Proton or SEAT cars. All cars *must* have a satisfactory Automobile Association (AA) report for which you pay.

The AA "Motorsure Car Component Insurance Scheme" must be arranged through the AA and Motability. This ensures against mechanical breakdown.

New and second hand cars: In addition to any extras you have to pay for, such as hand controls, AA Motorsure etc., all cars must have fully comprehensive insurance with a reputable company. Also an initial deposit will have to be paid. This will be the difference between the finance you get for surrendering your DLA (Mobility Component) or Supplement and the total cost of the vehicle you choose.

NOTE: Some cars are not available on hire purchase under this scheme, whether new or second hand. You can get full details from Motability.

Aid Vehicle Supplies (AVS)

Aid Vehicle Supplies is a commercial undertaking which offers to supply and finance cars for all disabled people and their families, subject to status. The applicant does not have to be in receipt of DLA (Mobility Component) nor need to be in employment, but must show proof of ability to pay.

AVS is able to supply virtually any new car, usually at a substantial discount, and also maintains a range of carefully selected used cars. Most adaptations can be fitted and included in the overall price. AVS will also liaise with Assessment Centres where necessary.

All cars are delivered to the customer's home address, and if required, the delivery driver will carry out a short demonstration of the vehicle and any adaptations fitted.

The finance terms will normally require a minimum deposit of 10% of the vehicle cost. Repayment periods of up to 5 years are available. Repayments are by bank standing order. Part exchange facilities are available. You can obtain explanatory leaflets and application forms direct from AVS.

Exemption from Vehicle Excise Duty (Road or Motor Tax)

If you receive DLA (Mobility Component), War Pensioners' Mobility Supplement or you drive an invalid carriage (trike) you may be entitled to exemption from road tax. This can be for a car you drive yourself or have driven for you.

If you receive DLA (Mobility Component) you will require a DLA 404 Entitlement Certificate. If you receive a War Pensioners' Mobility Supplement you will require an MPB 1266 Certificate. No certificate is required if you drive a trike.

You may also be able to claim exemption if you receive DLA (Care Component) which replaces the old Attendance Allowance, and you will require an MHS 330 Entitlement Certificate for this.

To obtain the explanatory leaflet V188 relating to the above, and for further advice, contact the Vehicle Enquiry Unit, DVLC, Swansea SA99 1BL (0792–772134). A Factsheet (no. 2) on exemption can also be obtained from RADAR, or alternatively you can get more information from the DDA, DDMC, DMF or Disability Scotland.

> NOTE: The exemption can only be claimed if the vehicle is used *solely by* or *only for* the purposes of carrying the disabled person concerned.

Relief from Car Tax and VAT

Motor vehicles designed or adapted to carry a disabled person in a wheelchair or on a stretcher, with no more than five other people, are exempt from car tax and free from VAT (zero-rated). The designed or adapted vehicle *must* include a permanently fitted hoist or ramp with suitable clamps to secure the wheelchair or stretcher. The disabled person can be the driver or passenger.

Other adaptations to cars, such as hand controls, *will not* qualify the car for car tax exemption. However, the cost of the controls etc. themselves, their installation and any repair and maintenance, are free from VAT.

For further details you should contact your local Customs and Excise Office (see your local Yellow Pages) and ask for leaflets VAT 701/7/86 and Notice 670. Also, a Factsheet (no.3) on this subject can be obtained from RADAR, or you can get more information from the DMF, Disability Scotland or MAVIS.

Insurance

It is well worth shopping around to find an insurance company which meets your needs best and most cheaply. Some firms do add premium loadings for disabled drivers, but many do not, because statistically disabled drivers are just as safe as able-bodied drivers and in many cases safer. The sort of car you have can make a big difference to the amount you pay, and it is well worth finding out about insurance ratings before you decide on which car to buy. You *must* state clearly your disability when taking out insurance. It is a legal requirement and you may be required to supply medical evidence. There are some insurance brokers who specialise in insurance for disabled drivers. For details contact MAVIS, RADAR (Factsheet No. 6) or alternatively you can contact the DDA, DDMC, DMF or Disability Scotland.

CARS AND DRIVING

Seat Belts

The law requires everyone, including disabled drivers and passengers, to wear seat belts in the front of a car and, since lst July 1991, passengers in the back of a car must also wear seat belts if they are fitted.

In exceptional cases a disabled person may, on medical grounds, be exempt from wearing a seat belt. The fact that a seat belt feels uncomfortable will not be accepted as a justification for exemption.

If you feel, for medical reasons, that you should not have to wear a seat belt, you should consult your doctor. You can get further information by writing to The Department of Transport, Room C18/21, 2 Marsham Street, London SW1P 3EB, or by contacting your Road Safety Officer through your local authority (in Scotland through your regional council offices). Alternatively you can contact MAVIS.

Choosing a Car and Adaptations

Choosing a car is a very personal affair and selecting the right one with suitable adaptations will obviously depend on the extent of your disability and experience. Because of this there are many variants to consider: seat heights, door widths, sill heights (including the boot or hatchback/estate door), layout of controls, 2-door or 4-door, height of door, power steering, automatic or manual transmission are just a selection.

Depending on your disability, driving adaptations start from the simple and relatively cheap single lever push/pull brake/accelerator control. These are fitted to automatic cars and to supply and fit would cost approximately £250 or less. For a manual car a full conversion would cost approximately £1,000 to supply and fit. If you are severely disabled there are other adaptations which use foot steering, which costs from around £1,200, or joy stick steering, which is very expensive, costing from around £5,000 to £10,000. There are also specialist vehicles available which can be driven from a wheelchair. In addition other adaptations such as a swivel seat or wheelchair hoist can also be fitted.

The wrong decision about adaptations could not only be expensive but also very impracticable. Because there is such a wide choice and range of adaptations to meet your individual needs, you are strongly recommended (especially if it is your first car) to seek advice from one of the Assessment Centres listed on page 81, some of which will have demonstration vehicles. Further information can be obtained from MAVIS, RADAR, DDA, DDMC or DMF.

▶ DRIVING LICENCES

Disabled drivers must take the same test and demonstrate the same standard of competence as everyone else. For the test the examiner will allocate approximately twice the usual time for a disabled driver. This takes into account the extra time that may be required to get to and into the car.

To obtain a licence you must use the standard application form (from most post offices). Again, you *must* state clearly your disability when applying for a licence. This is a legal requirement and you may be required to supply medical evidence.

Medical reports are considered by the Medical Adviser at the Driver and Vehicle Licensing Agency (DVLA) at Swansea, who will make a recommendation about the issue of a licence.

If your disability is stable and non-progressive you will normally be issued with a licence valid until your 70th birthday. Depending on your disability you may only be issued with a restricted licence (ie for 1, 2 or 3 years). After the licence fee has been paid on the initial application no further fees are required for the renewal of an expiring restricted period licence.

If you suffer from epilepsy, sudden attacks of disabling giddiness and fainting, or certain other medical conditions, you may be refused a licence unless the condition is under medical control and all legal requirements are satisfied.

If you already have a driving licence you must write to DVLA if you become disabled or if your condition gets worse. In certain circumstances you may have to retake the driving test. If you have a driving licence for a trike, you will need to have a separate provisional licence and to take the driving test if you want to drive an ordinary car, unless you have held a full licence for ordinary cars within the last 10 years.

For further information, Leaflet D100, "What You Need to Know About Driver Licencing", can be obtained from your local post office; or, alternatively, write to the Driver Enquiry Unit, DVLC, Swansea SA6 7JL (0792–772151). (DVLC is part of DVLA.)

▶ ASSESSMENT CENTRES

If you want to learn to drive or if you are thinking of returning to driving with a new or on-going disability, it is advisable to have an assessment of your driving ability and/or advice on the sort of controls and equipment you may need to overcome any physical limitations.

A list of non-commercial Assessment Centres is given on page 81. Further details of organisations offering assessment and advice are available in the booklet "Guide to Services in the UK Offering Advice, Information and Assessment to Disabled and Elderly Motorists", available from MAVIS.

▶ LEARNING TO DRIVE

There are quite a lot of driving schools with suitably adapted cars. MAVIS or Banstead Mobility Centre have a large list of schools and should be able to identify one or more within your area (as will Disability Scotland if you live in Scotland). Alternatively you can contact any of the other Assessment Centres listed on page 81, the DDA, DDMC or DMF.

▶ PARKING—ORANGE BADGE SCHEME

This Scheme provides a national system of parking concessions for people with severe disabilities who travel either as drivers or passengers, and for registered blind people and people with very severe upper limb disabilities who regularly drive a vehicle but cannot turn a steering wheel by hand. It allows badge holders to park closer to their destination. In England and Wales you can get an application form and explanatory leaflet about the Scheme from the Social Services Department of your local county, metropolitan district or

London borough council. In Scotland you should apply to the Chief Executive of your local regional or island council.

You will qualify for an Orange Badge if

- you received Mobility Allowance

- you receive the higher rate of the Mobility Component of the Disability Living Allowance

- you are registered blind

- you use a vehicle supplied by a Government Department

- you get a grant towards your own vehicle

- you receive a War Pensioners' Mobility Supplement

- you have a permanent and substantial disability which means you are unable to walk or have very considerable difficulty in walking. In this case your doctor may be asked to answer a series of questions to help the local authority determine whether you are eligible for a badge. People with a psychological disorder will not normally qualify unless their handicap causes very considerable difficulty in walking.

- you have a severe disability in both upper limbs, regularly drive a motor vehicle but cannot turn the steering wheel of a motor vehicle by hand even if that wheel is fitted with a turning knob.

The Scheme does not apply in the City of London, the City of Westminster, the London Borough of Kensington and Chelsea and part of the London Borough of Camden. For more detailed information see the Section on 'Driving in London: Parking' in Chapter 4, "Travelling In and Across London". It also does not apply on the road systems at some airports (eg: Heathrow).

Access to certain town centres may be prohibited or limited to vehicles with special permits. With these exceptions, the Orange Badge Scheme applies throughout England, Scotland and Wales.

Badge holders may park free of charge and without time limit at on-street parking meters, where there is 'pay and display' on-street parking and in time-limited waiting areas. Badge holders may also park on single or double yellow lines for up to 3 hours in England and Wales and without time limit in Scotland, except where there is a ban on loading or unloading.

There are restrictions on parking: for example, no parking is allowed in bus or cycle lanes during their hours of operation, where double white lines are in the centre of the road, and on the recently introduced Red Routes (at present only in London). On these routes vehicles are allowed to pick up and set down a disabled person, and there are limited parking bays, some of which are marked specifically for disabled people. These bays have various limited waiting times displayed.

Remember

- The Orange Badge is not a licence to park *anywhere*, and badge holders have the same obligations as other road users to ensure that they park safely and do not cause an obstruction. Vehicles which are parked dangerously or obstructively can be removed by the police.

- It is also *illegal* for able-bodied people to use a Badge. If they do so they are liable to a fine of up to £400, which increases to a maximum of £1,000 when the Criminal Justice Act 1991 is introduced, with the possible loss of the Orange Badge concession to the badge holder. The Scheme is a concession and *not a right* for disabled people.

- It is also illegal to drive a vehicle displaying an Orange Badge issued to an individual unless:

  i.   the badge holder is either driving or being carried as a passenger in the vehicle;

  ii. an able-bodied person is driving a vehicle along a road where a disabled persons concession is available to moving vehicles and he/she is on the way to collect a disabled person or, having set down the disabled person, is leaving the vicinity of the place where the disabled person was disembarked.

  The maximum fine for this offence is £400. This will be increased to £1,000 when the Criminal Justice Act 1991 comes into force.

- You can usually find out about parking facilities from local access guides (see Chapter 3 "Local Trips"). Many car parks, for example at stations or major shopping centres, have spaces reserved for people with disabilities. Some local authorities also provide designated on-street parking places near shopping centres etc. for people with disabilities. You must always display a valid Badge when occupying one of these spaces. If you have serious parking difficulties outside your home, some authorities may be able to provide parking places. It is well worth enquiring at your local social services office.

- Some other European countries allow disabled visitors to take advantage of the parking concessions provided for their own citizens by displaying the Orange Badge.

Further details of the Orange Badge Scheme, including reciprocal parking arrangements in Europe and details of exemptions from toll charges, can be obtained from the Department of Transport, Room C10/02, 2 Marsham Street, London SW1P 3EB. For Red Routes, write to the Department of Transport, Room C5/19A, at the same address. Alternatively any one of the Assessment Centres listed, Disability Scotland, DDA, DDMC or DMF should be able to give further information.

▶ MOTORING, ASSISTANCE AND SERVICES

On Motorways

You can drive on motorways in adapted cars but not in DSS trikes, with the exception of the Model 70, which was the last model produced. When on the motorway, if you need to pull on to the hard shoulder in an emergency, you should use your hazard warning lights,

CARS AND DRIVING

but they are not a call for other motorway users to come to your aid. If you use a wheelchair or have severe difficulty in walking you are strongly advised not to leave your car at all. Motorway emergency telephones are located too high for most people to reach from their wheelchair, because they have to be at a height which is safe to use by those not in a wheelchair. However, if you do choose to get out of your vehicle, you are strongly advised, because of the 'pull' of passing traffic, to leave enough space to get out of the car on the passenger side.

To attract people's attention, 'HELP' pennants and signs are available from various organisations such as the AA, National Breakdown, RAC, DDA, DDMC, DMF and RADAR, who will be able to advise on suppliers, or from the Cleveland Spastics Work and Welfare Centre, which manufactures them. If you are travelling alone you might wish to let the person at your destination know your estimated time of arrival and the exact route you are using.

For people who are hard of hearing and wear a hearing aid, inductive couplers are fitted to all motorway emergency telephones. Rather like radio, this device 'feeds' the receiver, without contact, into hearing aids which have a 'T' switch (all DSS models and some commercial ones). If you do not have a 'T' switch fitted to your hearing aid, or if you are profoundly deaf but can speak clearly, you should pick up the telephone and repeat 3 times your name, your disability and your problem. You should then replace the telephone and return to your car to wait for help. A patrol car will be sent out to assist you.

Motorway Services

All motorway service areas must have toilets which are accessible to people with disabilities, although the type of provision (male/female/unisex) and standards of size vary. Other facilities such as cafeterias, restaurants, shops are often different on the two sides of the motorway, sometimes with an over-bridge. You can get some idea of the access and facilities at motorway service areas from the "AA Guide for the Disabled Traveller" or the RAC's "On the Move".

On Other Roads

Local Access Guides

These may be able to provide you with information and they often give details of local garages, though you should bear in mind that more and more service stations are self-service. However, many do provide assistance for the disabled motorist, usually indicated by the standard 'wheelchair' sign.

Service Station Guides

Most service stations issue guides for travellers. These usually contain information on the whereabouts of the particular oil company garages, and may also contain details of other facilities, ie overnight stops, places to eat, toilets etc. There is also a National Key Scheme (NKS) in operation for toilets in the UK and abroad. For further information about this you should contact RADAR.

Roadside Stops

There are several well-known restaurant chains, eg Little Chef, Road Chef, AJ's Happy Eater, which have facilities for people with disabilities and produce handy maps or lists for the motorist giving their location. These can provide useful stops on a long journey. Also Forte Travelodge have rooms with facilities for disabled people in many parts of the UK. These provide cheap overnight accommodation currently costing £30 per room per night. A detailed list can be obtained from any Happy Eater or Little Chef restaurant, or alternatively by telephoning 0800–850950.

Motorail

You may find it helpful to use British Rail (BR) Motorail services for the 'long haul' part of your journey. BR staff will load your car. If, however, you travel in a wheelchair, whether or not you can transfer to a seat on the train, you will be unable to use the coaches on night Motorail services. More information about Motorail services can be found in Chapter 5 "Travelling Further Afield".

Breakdown and Recovery Services

The following organisations have a breakdown and recovery service specifically developed for disabled people:

Autohome LTD Nationwide Recovery Club (tel. 0604–232334).

Provides rescue, recovery, home start, plus other services such as road reports, routes, maps, Continental motoring requirements. Membership can be extended to the Continent. If you break down there is a special free Linkline. In addition, if you have not needed to use the breakdown service Autohome offers a no claims bonus.

Automobile Association (AA) (tel. 0345–500600 or 0252–24872).

Provides all normal services both in the UK and on the Continent. In addition an invalid carriage membership is available covering single-seater, three-wheeled motor propelled invalid vehicles. Discount membership is available to all Orange Badge holders and profoundly deaf people when paying for the full range of services by direct debit. Hearing impaired motorists, in possession of a Minicom, who break down can contact the AA direct on a free national breakdown number.

National Breakdown Recovery Club (tel. 0532–393939).

Provides all normal rescue and advice services. Two types of service are on offer: the Premiere and the Premiere Plus. If you join their scheme for disabled people both services cover travel in Europe at no extra charge. If you break down there is a free emergency phone number, and National Breakdown aim to reach all call-outs within the hour.

RAC Motoring Services (tel. 0272–238543).

"Response" is a package of services developed for disabled drivers. In addition to the Rescue, Recovery and At Home Services, further options will be coordinated by a Personal Incident Manager in each case where the vehicle cannot be repaired immediately. It also offers a Freephone emergency number and a Minicom phone number for hearing impaired drivers.

Remember

- There are several different ways of getting help with the cost of a car, whether or not you receive DLA (Mobility Component).

- You may also be eligible for exemption from Vehicle Excise Duty (road tax) and relief from VAT and car tax.

- Think carefully before deciding which adaptations to have fitted to your car and seek advice (eg from an Assessment Centre) first. A wrong decision could be an expensive and uncomfortable mistake!

- If you have severe walking difficulty you can apply for an Orange Badge to get parking concessions whether you are a car driver or a passenger.

- Even with an Orange Badge there are still some restrictions on where you may park.

- It is illegal to let an able-bodied person use your Orange Badge.

- National motoring organisations have developed breakdown and recovery services to cater for the needs of motorists with disabilities.

Useful Publications

"Motoring and Mobility for Disabled People". Published by the Royal Association for Disability and Rehabilitation (RADAR)

"On the Move – A Motorist's Guide for the Disabled Traveller". Published by the Royal Automobile Club (RAC).

"AA Guide for the Disabled Traveller". Published by the Automobile Association (AA).

▶ CONCESSIONS

Toll Bridges and Tunnels

In some cases owners/operators of bridges and tunnels will give concessions to disabled motorists provided certain requirements are met. This could mean exemption from Vehicle Excise Duty (road tax) or being in receipt of DLA (Mobility Component) etc. In some cases an application has to be made in advance to the relevant bridge/tunnel or local authority. Tickets or vouchers will be issued to successful applicants.

Concessions are normally available at the Severn, Erskine, Forth, Tay, Whitchurch and Whitney-on-Wye bridges and the Dartford and Tyne tunnels, without prior application. For the Clifton or Humber bridges and the Mersey tunnel an application must be made in advance to the addresses listed below:

- Clifton Suspension Bridge (B3124 West of Bristol)
  The Bridge Master, Clifton Suspension Bridge
  Leigh Woods, Bristol, Avon B58 3PA
  (Or obtain form direct from toll house)

- Humber Bridge
  Humber Bridge Board, Administration Building
  Ferriby Road, Hessle, North Humberside HU13 0JG
  0482–647161

- Mersey Tunnel
  George's Dock Building, George's Dock Way
  Pier Head, Liverpool L3 1DD
  051–236 8602

Concessions may well be available at other bridges and tunnels and if you regularly make a journey which involves a toll charge it is always worth enquiring first about possible concessions, particularly for less well known bridges and tunnels.

Further details on toll concessions can also be obtained from the AA, DDA, DDMC, RAC, RADAR or Disability Scotland.

▶ ASSESSMENT CENTRES

ENGLAND

Avon

Western Mobility Association
c/o 8 Streamside, Mangotsfield
Bristol, Avon
0272–561198

Berkshire

MAVIS:
Mobility Advice and Vehicle Information Service
Transport Research Laboratory
Old Wokingham Road
Crowthorne, Berks. RG11 6AU
0344–770456 (Minicom available)

Buckinghamshire

Stoke Mandeville Mobility Centre
Occupational Therapy Dept., Stoke Mandeville Hospital
Mandeville Road
Aylesbury, Bucks. HP21 8AL
0296–8411 ext.3271

Cornwall

Cornwall Friends Mobility Centre, Tehidy Hospital Grounds
Cambourne, Cornwall TR14 0SA
0209–710708

Derby

Derby Disabled Driving Centre, Kingsway Hospital
Kingsway, Derby DE3 3LZ
0332–371929

Devon

Devon Mobility Services, Devon Drivers Centre
Westpoint,
Clyst-St-Mary,
Exeter, Devon EX5 1DJ
0392–444773

Kent

S.E. Thames Regional Centre for Mobility Services
Preston Hall, Churchill Centre, Royal British Legion
Aylesford, Kent ME20 7NL
0622–717202 (9.30 a.m.-12.30 p.m.)

CARS AND DRIVING

Lancashire

Disabled Drivers Voluntary Advisory Service
18 The Roods, Warton,
nr. Carnforth, Lancs. LA5 9QG
0524–734195: Margaret Roden;
0524–823189: Chris Smith

Shropshire

Mobility Information Service, Unit 2A,
Atcham Estate
Upton Magna, Shrewsbury,
Shropshire SY4 4UG
0743–761889

Surrey

Banstead Mobility Centre, Damson Way,
Orchard Hill
Queen Mary's Avenue
Carshalton, Surrey SM5 4NR
081–770 1151

Tyne & Wear

The Mobility Centre, Regional Rehabilitation
Centre
Hunters Moor Hospital, Hunters Road
Newcastle-upon-Tyne,
Tyne & Wear NE2 4NR
091–221 0454

NORTHERN IRELAND

Disability Action
(formerly Northern Ireland Council on
Disability)
Driver Assessment Centre
2 Annadale Avenue, Belfast BT7 3JR
0232–491011

SCOTLAND

Edinburgh Driving Assessment Centre
Astley Ainslie Hospital, 133 Grange Loan
Edinburgh EH9 2HL
031–447 6271 ext.5211

WALES

West Glamorgan

Disabled Living Assessment Centre, St John's
Road
Manselton, Swansea,
W. Glamorgan SA5 8PC
0792–580161

South Glamorgan

Wales Disabled Drivers Assessment Centre
18 Plasnewydd, Whitchurch
Cardiff, S. Glamorgan CF4 1NR
0222–615276

Rookwood Driving Assessment Centre
Rookwood Hospital, Fairwater Road
Llandaff, S. Glamorgan CF5 2YN
0222–566281 (ext.3776 a.m. or 3755 p.m.)

▶ USEFUL CONTACTS

Autohome Ltd
202–204 Kettering Road,
Northampton NN1 4HE
0604–232336

Automobile Association (AA)
Fanum House, Basingstoke,
Hants. RG21 2EA
0345–500600

Aid Vehicle Supplies (AVS)
Hockley Industrial Centre, Hooley Lane
PO Box 26, Redhill, Surrey RH1 6JF
0737–770030/32, Fax 0737–778288

Cleveland Spastics Work and Welfare
Service
Acklam Road
Middlesbrough
Cleveland TS5 4EG
0642–818854

Disabled Drivers Association (DDA)
Ashwellthorpe Hall, Ashwellthorpe,
Norfolk NR16 1EX
0508–41449

Disabled Drivers Motor Club (DDMC)
Cottingham Way, Thrapston,
Northamptonshire NN14 4PL
0832–734724

Disabled Motorists Federation (DMF)
Unit 2a, Atcham Estate, Upton Magna
Shrewsbury, Shropshire SY4 4UG
0743–761889

Disability Scotland
Princes House, 5 Shandwick Place
Edinburgh EH2 4RG
031–229 8632

DVLC Enquiry Unit (DVLA)
Swansea SA99 1BL
0792–772134

DVLC Driver Enquiry Unit (DVLA)
Swansea SA6 7JL
0792–772151

Department of Transport (DoT) Disability
    Unit
Room S10/21, 2 Marsham Street, London
    SW1P 3EB
071–276 5257 (Minicom 071–276 4973)

    About Seat Belts (the new law) write to
        Rm C18/21; tel 071–276 6554

    For Orange Badge details write to Rm
        C10/02; tel 071–276 6291

    For Red Routes details write to Rm
        C5/19A; tel 071–276 6103

Mobility Advice and Vehicle Information
    Service (MAVIS)
Transport Research Laboratory
Old Wokingham Road
Crowthorne, Berks. RG11 6AU
0344–770456 (Minicom available)

Motability
Gate House, West Gate, The High
Harlow, Essex CM20 1HR
0279–635666

National Breakdown Recovery Club
Cote Lane, Leeds, W. Yorkshire LS99 2LZ
0532–393939

Royal Assocation for Disability and
    Rehabilitation (RADAR)
25 Mortimer Street, London W1N 8AB
071–637 5400

Royal Automobile Club (RAC)
PO Box 700, Spectrum, Pond Street
Bristol, Avon BS99 1RB
0272–232444 (General Enquiries)
0272–232340 (Membership Enquiries)

7. TRAVELLING ABROAD

TRAVELLING ABROAD

USEFUL CONTACTS **101**
- Preparations Before You Go
- Motoring Organisations
- Hiring Hand-Controlled Cars to Take Abroad
- Hiring Hand-Controlled Cars in North America
- Ferry Companies
- Rail Travel In Europe
- Air Travel

▶ **PREPARATIONS BEFORE YOU GO**

Insurance

You should make sure you have a good insurance policy when you travel abroad. Most travel agents can supply comprehensive policies but there can be a problem for disabled people. Some policies do not cover claims arising from a "pre-existing medical condition or defect", ie claims arising from your disability. You should check that any travel insurance you are offered does NOT contain such a clause.

There are insurance companies which specialise in policies for disabled people and which offer policies that do not contain this exclusion. You can get information about these companies from the Royal Association for Disability and Rehabilitation (RADAR), Holiday Care Service and TRIPSCOPE.

Medical Preparations

You should always check any special health requirements for the country you are visiting. Vaccination may be required, or advisable, against certain diseases, more especially for third world countries. However, vaccination may not be possible for people with known allergies or certain medical conditions. If this applies to you, you can get an Exemption Certificate from your GP or consultant well in advance of your date of travel.

British Airways have a number of immunisation centres throughout Britain (you do not have to be flying with British Airways, or even to be travelling abroad by air, to use this service). They can give vaccinations and provide Exemption Certificates as necessary (you will have to pay, but no charge is made for information). Their main centre in Central London is fully (w) accessible and can give details of the location of the other centres throughout Britain.

If you have a particular condition eg: diabetes mellitus or multiple sclerosis AND you think you might need emergency attention when abroad, check whether your disability association produces a card for you to carry with you, which gives details of your disability in foreign languages.

If you are travelling to a European Community (EC) country AND you are a UK National you may get free or reduced rate emergency medical treatment while you are there. Only emergency treatment is covered, which is provided on the same basis as for its own nationals. To benefit from this, you will need a form E111, which is available from post offices.

86

You can get full details of health care and advice for travellers abroad in two free booklets published by the Department of Health. Copies can be obtained by telephoning 0800–555777 any time, free of charge. They are "Health Advice For Travellers Outside the European Community" (T3) and "Health Advice For Travellers In The European Community" (T2) also available at post offices and containing form E111.

Remember

- Make sure you have the right travel insurance.
- Seek medical advice well before your travel date.
- If you are taking medication, carry enough with you to last your stay.

▶ TAKING YOUR CAR ABROAD

If you have your own car, driving may be the easiest way of travelling abroad in Europe. The advantages are:

- few problems with heavy luggage;
- room to take portable aids with you;
- freedom to plan your own routes;
- freedom to travel at a pace which suits you; and
- freedom to go 'off the beaten track'.

The disadvantages are:

- getting accustomed to unfamiliar driving rules abroad;
- less immediate help if things go wrong (especially in more remote areas); and
- more stress or anxiety for the driver.

If you decide to take your car abroad, the following motoring organisations can give helpful advice:

The Automobile Association (AA) and the Royal Automobile Club (RAC) particularly for help with route planning and maps.

The Disabled Drivers' Association (DDA), The Disabled Drivers' Motor Club (DDMC) and The Disabled Motorists' Federation (DMF) especially for information about concessions on cross-Channel ferries.

Essential Documents and Equipment

You should be aware of the documents and equipment which you should carry with you when driving abroad. Detailed information can be obtained from the motoring organisations or your insurance company, but the key items to remember are:

- green card
- driving licence (UK or International)
- vehicle registration document (or log book) OR vehicle hire certificate (VE103A)

- GB sticker
- warning triangle
- two wing mirrors
- headlight beam converter
- first-aid kit
- spare headlight bulbs
- fire extinguisher

Whilst *all* of these items are useful to have with you when driving abroad, many of them are compulsory for some European countries.

Hiring a Car in Britain to Take Abroad

Many hire companies will allow you to hire a car in Britain to drive abroad in Europe, but you will be charged additional insurance premiums and you may have to take out special recovery service insurance with one of the motoring organisations.

Hiring A Car With Hand Controls To Take Abroad

It is possible to hire cars fitted with hand controls in Britain to drive abroad. The companies which offer this service are:

Hertz Car Rentals

Mobility Car Rentals

Perrys of Edgware

Rod Surrage Appeal Fund

You may be required to take out special recovery service insurance with one of the motoring organisations.

Hiring A Hand-Controlled Car When You Are Abroad

You may wish to hire a hand-controlled car once you have arrived abroad. It is possible to do this in a number of countries. The disability motoring organisations, RADAR or TRIPSCOPE will have details. If you are travelling to North America, this can be arranged before you go, whether you wish to have the car-hire organised as part of a holiday package or want to travel independently. Companies which can offer the hire of hand-controlled cars or specially adapted vehicles as part of an all-in holiday package are:

Assistance Travel Services Ltd

Northwest 'Holiday America'

Threshold Travel Ltd

If you want to travel independently in the USA your car-hire can be arranged in advance by:

Avis Rent-A-Car

Hertz Car Rentals

Lindo's Rent-a-Car

If you cannot hire a hand-controlled car in the country you are visiting, you can hire a conversion kit in the UK to take with you. This will convert an ordinary car to one which can be hand-controlled. If you do this you MUST:

● *have the kit fitted by a skilled fitter*; AND

● *check the insurance arrangements with the dealer whose car you are hiring.* **Failure to do this could invalidate your insurance.**

Reciprocal Parking Arrangements

Europe

Reciprocal parking arrangements are available for Orange Badge holders in most West European countries, although no formal schemes exist in Norway, Spain or the Republic of Ireland and there are no schemes at all in Gibraltar or Greece. A leaflet entitled "Orange Badge Scheme: Reciprocal Parking Arrangements for Disabled and Blind People in Europe" is available free of charge from the Department of Transport.

Where there are no formal reciprocal arrangements in Europe, you should take your Orange Badge with you and notify the local police when you arrive. This should be enough for you to obtain local parking concessions.

Australia, Canada, New Zealand, USA.

Take your Orange Badge with you and notify the local police when you arrive. This should be enough for you to obtain local parking concessions.

Remember

● Allow plenty of time to prepare for your trip.
● Consult one of the motoring organisations before you go.
● The ten essential documents and pieces of equipment.
● Take your Orange Badge with you.

▶ CROSSING THE CHANNEL

If you are travelling by sea to another European country you will have to decide which ferry route to use. The main considerations are:

● British port facilities;
● Continental port facilities;
● facilities on board the ferry;
● concessions offered by the ferry company; and
● how the Channel crossing fits in with your overall route.

Two publications which may help you make the best decision are: "The AA Guide for the Disabled Traveller", and the RAC's "On the Move: A Motorist's Guide for the Disabled Traveller".

TRAVELLING ABROAD

British Port Facilities

The range of facilities available to people with disabilities varies considerably from port to port. You should consider such things as:

- the distance from railway station, car park/queueing area to the terminal building;
- provision of lifts/ramps in the terminal building; and
- provision and location of (w) accessible toilets.

Generally, facilities are particularly good at:

Dover	Newcastle
Dover Hoverport	Portsmouth
Felixstowe	Ramsgate
Harwich	Sheerness
Hull	

For people with disabilities using Dover, there is a useful free leaflet, "Happy to Help". This guide is available from: The Corporate Affairs Department, Dover Harbour Board, Cambridge Terrace, Dover, Kent CT17 9BJ. Tel. 0304–240400 ext. 4807.

There are no (w) accessible toilets at Newhaven, Plymouth or Southampton, and at Newhaven there are two steps to the terminal building.

Details can be obtained from the Port Manager or the ferry company if your travel or booking agent cannot give you the advice you need.

If you are travelling by car and do not wish to use any of the port facilities, you should be able to drive straight on or off the ferry without having to get out of your car, subject to Customs and Immigration requirements (but you will not be allowed to stay in your car once on board the ferry).

RADAR has published a guide entitled "Access at the Channel Ports: A Guide for Disabled People", containing useful information on port and ferry facilities (but it is based on research done in 1985/6 so check for any alterations since then).

Continental Port Facilities

Facilities also vary at Continental ports, so check with your travel/booking agent or ferry company. (The panel on page 97 gives a brief summary.)

Ferries–Help With Getting on Board

If you are not travelling by car, access to the ship is usually by ramp, which can be steep. There are sometimes steps as well. You should give the ferry company as much notice as possible of the help you will need in boarding and disembarking (it may be easier for you to use the lift via the car deck, and a wheelchair can be made available if you need one).

If you are travelling by car, the ferry company can arrange for your car to be parked on board near the lift, and can help you get to the passenger accommodation. You must arrive in plenty of time, and let the ferry company know well in advance what time you will arrive at the port.

Ferries—Facilities On Board

Many ferry companies operate fleets with an increasing number of ships which are equipped with lifts and (w) accessible toilets. Some older ships which are only partially accessible are still in service, so check with your travel/booking agent or the ferry company before booking. The panel on page 98 summarises the facilities available on the main routes.

Conditions of Carriage

If you are travelling in a wheelchair, have severe walking difficulties, are blind or partially sighted, many ferry companies would like you to give advance notice, and be accompanied by an able-bodied companion. Most offer this as advice, so that the appropriate help can be given where needed, rather than making it a condition. Check with the ferry company or your travel agent for any conditions which may apply.

Concessions

Most ferry companies offer concessions to customers with disabilities (but some are not available in the peak summer months). Some offer free or reduced-price car transport (passengers pay the full fare). You should be either a member of the DDA/DDMC/DMF or registered disabled with your local authority. You will need either a form (supplied by the ferry company) or a letter signed by the motoring organisation (who will make a small charge for this) or your local Social Services Department. You can get more details from the ferry company, disabled drivers' organisation or your travel agent.

Remember

- Choose a route that gives you the best *overall* journey. Think about driving distance, port and ferry facilities.
- Give the ferry company advance notice of your date and time of travel.
- Let the ferry company know of any assistance you need.
- Check whether you are entitled to any concessions.

▶ TRAVELLING ABROAD BY COACH

The facilities for people with disabilities who want to travel to Europe by coach *on scheduled services* are very poor. Coaches usually have several entry steps and are not directly accessible to people in wheelchairs (unless a lift has been fitted). However, some companies operate inclusive coach tours to Europe with fully (w) accessible coaches. Details can be found in Chapter 8 "Holidays" on page 108.

▶ RAIL TRAVEL IN EUROPE

In Western Europe, facilities for disabled people who wish to travel by rail are extremely varied. They range from countries where many trains and stations are fully accessible to those where there are no special facilities or arrangements at all.

One major difference between railways in the UK and those in most other European countries is that the level of the platforms is usually much lower at stations on the

Continent. So whilst getting from street level on to the station itself may often be easier than in the UK, getting from the platform into the train (and vice-versa) is usually more difficult, with two or three steep steps up into the train. Increasingly, facilities are being provided and help is being made available for passengers travelling in wheelchairs.

Always check the facilities and help available well in advance of your journey, especially if you plan to travel through more than one country, when you will need to coordinate assistance between different national railway companies. The **British Rail (BR) International** office in London is very helpful and can arrange for assistance on the British part of any rail journey (but you will have to make any arrangements for help abroad direct with the rail company concerned). Bookings and reservations can usually be made through BR International or BR Travel Centres.

Concessions

There is no standard concession for disabled passengers throughout European countries, so you should check with the railway company of the country concerned (or BR International) before you go.

Holders of a **British Rail Senior Railcard** can obtain discounts on Continental rail travel by purchasing a **Rail Europe Senior Card**. The discount applies to Continental rail tickets bought either in Britain or at stations in any of the European countries covered by the scheme.

A blind person buying an international rail ticket is entitled to an identical ticket to the same destination, free of charge, for one accompanying passenger.

Remember

- Check the facilities or help available before you book.
- Facilities vary considerably between different countries.

For further information contact the railway company of the country concerned before you go. Some produce booklets in English and many have offices in the UK. They are listed under Useful Contacts at the end of this chapter.

▶ INTERNATIONAL AIR TRAVEL

Air travel is becoming increasingly accessible for people with disabilities, but you do need to plan well ahead to be sure of a trouble-free journey. You need to think about:

- Who will have to know of any special help you will need;
- Getting to and from the airport;
- What help you will need at the airport;
- Any special arrangements you will need on the aircraft; and
- Concessions or extra charges which may apply.

Information Before You Go

Passengers with disabilities are generally treated no differently from any other passenger by the airlines, but where necessary special arrangements can be made. However, there are conditions which airports and airlines have to observe on the advice of the Civil Aviation Authority (CAA) and the International Air Transport Association (IATA) in the interests of the safety and health of ALL passengers.

It is important to let the airline know in advance of any special needs you have. For example, if you are taking special equipment such as dialysis equipment or a respirator, you will need to give the airline advice on how to handle it. If you are likely to need oxygen during the flight, special arrangements will have to be made. You can get free advice and information on special arrangements which can be made from the British Airways Invalid Passenger Unit at Heathrow Airport.

To help you get the assistance you need at the airport and on the aircraft you may need to complete a special form called an **"Incapacitated Passengers Handling Advice (INCAD)"** which replaces the previous Standard Medical Information Form (MEDIF). Check with your travel agent or airline (who can supply the form) as this is not always needed.

Part 1 has to be filled in by your travel agent, or whoever makes the booking. It covers:

● any equipment you will be taking with you;

● help you will need at the airport;

● help getting on and off the aircraft; and

● help during the flight and in an emergency evacuation.

For most disabled people this is all that is needed formally, and special arrangements will then be made; but it is always wise to double-check with the airline direct, before you go.

Part 2 is a medical clearance. It is usually needed only if you have an illness or disease, or if you are recovering from an operation. Your doctor has to complete this part. Airlines can refuse your booking if your medical condition might jeopardise the health or safety of other passengers or the crew. If your medical condition might adversely affect you during the flight you should let the airline know in advance about what to do, and also mention it to the cabin crew, once on board. Cabin staff are trained to deal with medical emergencies, but are not expected to undertake routine medical/nursing care. They can insist you are accompanied by someone who can provide this care for you.

Frequent Air Travellers

It would be worth getting a **"Frequent Travellers Medical Card (FREMEC)"** if the following apply to you:

● you have a disability, AND
● you travel frequently by air, AND

- you have a stable medical condition
  (in the opinion of an airline Medical Officer).

A FREMEC saves you the trouble of completing an INCAD form each time you fly and is issued free of charge. It is accepted by most airlines which are members of IATA. Even if you do have this card you should still let the airline know your disability and what help you need each time you travel. You can apply for a FREMEC from the Medical Department of any of the major IATA airlines.

Taking Your Wheelchair With You

It is possible to take your wheelchair with you when you fly, but you may not sit in your wheelchair on board the plane. Most airlines accept powered wheelchairs with dry-cell batteries, provided the battery is disconnected and the leads insulated. Some airlines will not accept those fitted with wet-cell batteries and those that do, insist that the acid be drained, or that the battery be sealed in one of their own leak-proof packing boxes.

Getting to the Airport

It may be convenient for you to fly from your local, or nearest airport, but this is not possible for flights to all destinations or for many charter flights. If you are flying from a local airport you may be able to arrange for a family member or friend to drive you there. Otherwise one of the organisations mentioned in Chapter 3 "Local Trips" might be able to provide transport.

If you are travelling to the airport by car you should check the arrangements for 'setting down' outside the airport terminal building, and the car parking arrangements, with the airport.

London's Heathrow Airport provides a (w) accessible bus service between the long-stay car parks and each terminal. You have to notify the long-stay car park reception on your arrival that you wish to use this service. On your return the bus can be summoned by using the special telephone adjacent to the long-stay car park bus stop outside each terminal.

At London's Gatwick Airport Orange Badge holders may park in the short-stay car parks at the much cheaper long-stay car park rates. Disabled passengers using the special bays in the short-stay car parks may summon assistance by using the telephones next to the bay, but it is better to contact the main car park office in advance, giving them details of any assistance you will need.

At London's Stansted Airport *all* buses between the long-stay car park and the terminal building are (w) accessible.

The panel on page 99 describes the public transport links to London's airports which may be more accessible for people with disabilities.

At the Airport

Most major airports in the UK publish a booklet about the facilities that are available and how to obtain the help you may need. You should be able to get one from the airport's information department.

One of the most confusing parts of the journey can be between your arrival at the airport and your finding the right check-in desk. Airport information staff can help and your airline or its handling agent can arrange for you to be met at the airport if you let them know in advance. They will help you right the way through the airport if necessary, from assisting with your luggage and checking in to taking you through security and passport control to the aircraft boarding point. A wheelchair can be provided if you need one.

Heathrow and Gatwick Airports both have a Travel Care Centre with staff who can help you at the airport in this way. They just need to know details of either your arrival at the airport or your return flight and what help you will need. Heathrow Travel Care publishes a booklet which contains useful information about travelling through the airport. "A Guide to Heathrow Airport for People With Special Needs" is available free of charge from Heathrow Travel Care as well as from RADAR or TRIPSCOPE.

If You Are Travelling With Your Own Wheelchair

This help at the airport can also be made available if you are travelling in a wheelchair. You must make arrangements in advance. After checking-in you should be able to stay in your own wheelchair until boarding the plane, but some airlines require you to transfer to an airline wheelchair right away, depending on their procedures for loading your wheelchair on to the aircraft. (The wheelchair has to be carried in the baggage hold of the aircraft.)

Usually you will be taken on board first and taken off the plane last. You may be lifted on to the plane by staff, using a carrying seat, or be taken in a special vehicle and lifted with a high-lift loading vehicle. You will be transferred to your seat on the aircraft either by lifting or by means of a small aisle wheelchair.

If You Are Blind Or Partially Sighted

The Royal National Institute for the Blind (RNIB) has produced "Plane Easy", a tape and leaflet giving information about air travel and assistance at UK airports for blind people. It is also available in braille.

If you are blind or partially sighted and travelling alone you MUST be helped through the various stages to and from the aircraft. At Gatwick you must enlist the help of your airline handling agent, as flight announcements are not made through the public address system.

If you are taking your guide dog with you, the dog will have to travel in the hold and you will be charged the air-cargo rate for it. On return from any foreign country the normal six month quarantine period also applies to guide dogs! You should contact the Guide Dogs for the Blind Association first, to discuss the implications this raises for care of your dog on the flight, whilst abroad, and for arrangements whilst it is in quarantine on your return to the UK.

If You Are Hearing-Impaired

If you have hearing difficulties and are travelling unaccompanied you should let the airline know in advance so that staff can help with announcements. You should also tell the cabin staff, on boarding the aircraft, that you have a hearing impairment.

If you wear a hearing aid you can, by switching it to the 'T' position, use public telephones at airports in the usual way. Heathrow and Gatwick Airport Information Desks have induction loops fitted and there is a special (induction loop) area in the departure lounges. If you switch your hearing aid to the 'T' position there, you will be able to hear information through the public address system. (NB: Flight announcements are NOT made at Gatwick Airport, except in the satellite lounge where induction loops have been fitted.)

On the Aircraft

If requested, airlines will try to allocate a seat with additional legroom, and close to the toilet. However, you will not be allowed to sit in seats next to the emergency exits (where there is extra legroom) because access to these exits has to be kept free at all times. Generally aircraft on long-haul flights have roomier seating than those on short-haul or charter flights. Some seats on certain aircraft have lift-up armrests to make access easier.

Toilet facilities vary between aircraft, even between those of the same airline. Airline staff may assist you to the toilet (using an aisle chair if available) but are not allowed to assist you in the toilet as they are classified as food handlers. Some planes now have accessible toilets, so you should check with the airline beforehand on the toilet facilities available.

If you are anxious about toilet arrangements you should consider incontinence garments. Some disability organisations such as the DLF and Spinal Injuries Association (SIA) have their own incontinence advisers, and a booklet called "Personal Toilet On Long Flights" is available from the DLF.

If you wish to compare the various facilities offered by different airlines you should contact the **Access To The Skies Committee** (c/o RADAR) which has a complete database of this information.

Concessions and Extra Charges

On international flights the only concession is usually free carriage of a folding wheelchair. Airline help is usually free unless you have exceptional needs at the airport (eg you have to travel on a stretcher). Extra charges will also be made if you need to occupy more than one seat on the plane.

Remember

- Whatever your needs, check with the airline before you book.
- Allow plenty of time to get to the airport.
- Make sure you will have the help you need on your return.

For further information there are two useful booklets: "Care In The Air": Advice for Handicapped Travellers", and "Flight Plan: Hints for Airline Passengers". Both can be obtained, free, from the Air Transport Users' Committee.

▶ FACILITIES AT CONTINENTAL PORTS

PORT	ACCESS TO TERMINAL BUILDING	ACCESS IN TERMINAL BUILDING	(W) ACCESSIBLE TOILETS
Boulogne	Level	Level	Yes
Boulogne Hoverport	Level	Level	Yes
Caen	Level	Level	Yes
Calais	Level	Level	Yes
Calais Hoverport	2 Steps	Level	Yes
Cherbourg	Ramped	Level	No
Dieppe	2 Steps	2 Floors/ Many steps	No
Le Havre	Level	Level	No
Roscoff	Level	2 Steps	Yes
St Malo	Level	Level	Yes
Hook of Holland	4 Steps	Level	No
Ostend	Travelator to 1st Floor (1 in 10 slope) for non-car travellers		Yes (in the Jetfoil Term.)
Rotterdam	Level	Level	Yes
Santander	Steps	Level	No
Vlissingen (Flushing)	2 Steps	Level	No
Zeebrugge (P&O Term.)	Level	Level	Yes

TRAVELLING ABROAD

▶ **FACILITIES ON CROSS-CHANNEL AND OTHER FERRIES**

ROUTE	OPERATOR AND FACILITIES
Newcastle—Bergen—Stavanger	**Color Line:** MS Venus has adapted 3-berth cabins, (w) accessible toilets, lifts to all decks.
Hull—Rotterdam—Zeebrugge	**North Sea Ferries:** Adapted cabins with wide doors, (w) accessible toilets, lifts to all decks.
Felixstowe—Zeebrugge	**P&O European Ferries:** Adapted cabins on 'Nordic Ferry', 'Baltic Ferry'; (w) accessible toilets, lift.*
Harwich—Esbjerg	**Scandinavian Seaways:** (w) accessible cabins, lifts to all decks, good general access.
Harwich—Hook of Holland	**Sealink Stena Line:** older ferries only partially (w) accessible but excellent facilities on the 'Sylvia Regina'.
Sheerness—Vlissingen (Flushing)	**Olau Line:** 'Olau Hollandia' and 'Olau Britannia' have (w) accessible cabins, adapted toilets, handrails for visually impaired passengers, and lifts to all decks.
Ramsgate—Dunkirk	**Sally Line:** 'Sally Star' has adapted cabins with wide doors but 6cm. door sills; (w) accessible toilet and lift to all decks. 'Sally Sky' has limited lift access. Both have restaurant menus in braille.
Dover—Calais	**Sealink Stena Line:** older ferries only partially (w) accessible but excellent facilities on the 'Fantasia', 'Fiesta', 'Cote d'Azur'.
Dover—Calais	**P&O European Ferries:** 'Pride of Dover', 'Pride of Calais' fully (w) accessible.
—Boulogne	'Pride of Canterbury', 'Pride of Hythe' (w) accessible toilets and lift to main deck (but not to Club Class).*
—Zeebrugge	'Pride of Bruges' has best facilities.*
—Ostend	P&O's Belgian partner **RMT** operates some ships without (w) accessible toilets pending refurbishment and introduction of a new luxury ferry.
Newhaven—Dieppe	**Sealink Stena Line:** older ferries only partially (w) accessible but excellent facilities on the 'Champs Elysees'.
*P&O European Ferries:	On all ferries the lift from car deck to passenger deck is a service lift. Advance notice is essential.

Portsmouth—Le Havre	**P&O European Ferries:** adapted cabins, (w) accessible toilets and lifts on the 'Pride of Le Havre' and 'Pride of Hampshire'.*
—Cherbourg	'Pride of Winchester' and 'Pride of Cherbourg' have adapted cabins, (w) accessible toilets and lift.*
Portsmouth—Caen —St Malo	**Brittany Ferries:** good access on all ships.
Southampton—Cherbourg	**Sealink Stena Line:** older ferries are only partially accessible.
Poole—Cherbourg Plymouth—Roscoff —Santander	**Brittany Ferries:** good access on all ships. The 'Bretagne' (Plymouth—Santander) has adapted cabins.
Swansea—Cork	**Swansea Cork Ferries:** (March-October) one ship with adapted (w) accessible toilets and lift to all decks.
Pembroke—Rosslare	**B&I Line:** (w) accessible (service) lift to passenger deck; (w) accessible toilet and cabins with wide doors.
Fishguard—Rosslare Holyhead—Dun Laoghaire	**Sealink Stena Line:** older ferries are only partially accessible.
Holyhead—Dublin	**B&I Line:** (w) accessible (service) lift to passenger deck; (w) accessible toilet and cabins with wide doors.
***P&O European Ferries:**	On all ferries the lift from car deck to passenger deck is a service lift. Advance notice is essential.

▶ CATAMARAN SERVICES

Dover—Calais —Boulogne	**Hoverspeed:** no longer use hovercraft. Fully accessible Catamaran Seacats are used; (w) accessible toilets.

N.B. On the Boulogne service there is (November 1991) poor (w) access at Dover and pending improvements this will involve some manual handling of wheelchairs by staff.

▶ GETTING TO LONDON'S AIRPORTS BY PUBLIC TRANSPORT

Heathrow

London Transport (LT) runs the 'Airbus' (w) accessible bus service between Central London and all four terminals at Heathrow. There are two routes:

● A1 between Heathrow and Victoria Coach and Railway Stations via South Kensington; and

- A2 between Heathrow and Russell Square via Bayswater, Marble Arch and Euston.

The journey lasts 50–60 minutes and the service on both routes is operated at 20–30 minute intervals throughout the day, 7 days per week. Both routes pass close to many Central London hotels and both connect with LT's Stationlink service at either Victoria or Euston. Stationlink is a (w) accessible bus service which links the main London British Rail (BR) termini on a one-way circular route. It is an hourly service operated throughout the day, 7 days per week. Two leaflets, "Airport/Hotel Transfer" and "Stationlink", are available free of charge from LT's Unit for Disabled Passengers.

(W) accessible taxis are also available at the airport taxi ranks. The fare to and from Central London is much more expensive than for other public transport services, but the taxi may be more convenient.

Gatwick

BR operates the (w) accessible Gatwick Express from London's Victoria station every 15 minutes throughout the day, every day. The journey takes 30 minutes and you do not need to give advance notice.

If you are travelling to Gatwick from north of London, or from the Brighton area, it may be more convenient to use BR's (w) accessible Thameslink service which runs between Bedford and Brighton via Luton, St. Albans, Central London and Gatwick. The only (w) accessible Central London stations on this route are City Thameslink and London Bridge.

Stansted

BR operates a half-hourly (w) accessible express service between London's Liverpool Street Station and Stansted, taking 45 minutes.

You do not need to give BR advance notice before using this service.

Luton

Luton is served by a BR (w) accessible InterCity service from London's St. Pancras Station, or by the (w) accessible Thameslink service (see entry on Gatwick, above).

London City Airport

Situated to the East of London, the public transport links are not well suited to wheelchair access. This will improve when the Docklands Light Railway (DLR) extension is completed. It is due to open by 1993. In the meantime, if you need (w) accessible public transport to or from Central London it is probably best to take a (w) accessible taxi.

► USEFUL CONTACTS

TRAVELLING ABROAD

Preparations Before You Go

British Airways Travel Clinic
156 Regent Street
London W1R 5TA
071–439 9584

Holiday Care Service
2 Old Bank Chambers
Station Road
Horley, Surrey RH6 9UY
0293–774535

Royal Association For Disability And
    Rehabilitation (RADAR)
25 Mortimer Street
London W1N 8AB
071–637 5400

TRIPSCOPE
63 Esmond Road
London W4 1JE
081–994 9294 (Minicom available)

AND

Pamwell House
160 Pennywell Road
Bristol BS5 0TX
0272–494094

TRAVELLING ABROAD BY CAR

Motoring Organisations

The Automobile Association (AA)
Fanum House
Basingstoke, Hants. RG21 2EA
0345–500600

The Disabled Drivers' Association (DDA)
Ashwellthorpe Hall
Ashwellthorpe
Norwich, Norfolk NR16 1EX
0508–41449

The Disabled Drivers' Motor Club (DDMC)
Cottingham Way
Thrapston, Northants. NN14 4PL
0832–734724

The Disabled Motorists' Federation (DMF)
Unit 2a, Atcham Industrial Estate
Upton Magna,
Shrewsbury, Shropshire SY4 4UG
0743–761889

The Royal Automobile Club (RAC)
RAC Motoring Services
PO Box 700
Spectrum
Bond Street
Bristol, Avon BS99 1RB
0272–232444 (General Enquiries)
0272–232340 (Membership Enquiries)

RAC European Service
RAC House
PO Box 100
South Croydon CR2 6XW
081–686 0088

Hiring Hand-Controlled Cars to Take Abroad

Hertz Car Rentals
Radnor House
1272 London Road, Norbury
London SW16 4XW
081–679 1799

Mobility Car Rentals
74 Mandeville Road
Enfield, Middlesex EN3 6SL
0992–87462

Perrys of Edgware
51 High Street
Edgware, Middlesex
081–952 2353

Rod Surrage Appeal Fund
1 Johnston Green
Guildford, Surrey GU2 6XS
0483–233640

TRAVELLING ABROAD

Hiring Hand-Controlled Cars in North America

AVIS Rent-A-Car
International Sales & Marketing
AVIS House, Park Road
Bracknell, Berks. RG12 2EW
0344–426644

Assistance Travel Service Ltd
1 Quarry View Road, Tank Lane
Purfleet, Essex RM16 1TA
0708–803198

Lindo's Rent-A-Car
Paddon House
12 Stortford Road
Great Dunmow, Essex
(Freefone) 0800–252897

Northwest 'Holiday America'
PO Box 45
Bexhill-on-Sea, East Sussex TN40 1PY
0424–732777

Threshhold Travel Ltd
80 Newry Street
Banbridge, County Down
Northern Ireland BT32 3HA
0820–662954

TRAVELLING ABROAD BY SHIP

Ferry Companies

B & I Line PLC
Passenger Office
Reliance House
Water Street
Liverpool L2 8TP
051–227 3131

Brittany Ferries
The Brittany Centre
Wharf Road
Portsmouth, Hants. PO2 8RU
0705–827701

OR
Brittany Ferries
Millbay Docks
Plymouth, Devon PL1 3EW
0752–221321

Color Line
Tyne Commission Quay
North Shields
Tyne and Wear NE29 6EA
091–296 1313

Hoverspeed Ltd
International Hoverport
Western Docks
Dover, Kent CT17 9TG
0304–240101
OR
081–554 7061 (London)
021–236 2190 (Birmingham)
061–228 1321 (Manchester)

North Sea Ferries Ltd
King George Dock
Hedon Road
Hull, North Humberside HU9 5QA
0482–795141

Olau Line (UK) Ltd
104 Anchor Lane
Sheerness Docks
Kent ME12 1SN
0795–580010

P & O European Ferries
Channel House, Channel View Road
Dover, Kent CT17 9TJ
0304–203388

Sally Line Ltd
Argyle Centre
York Street
Ramsgate, Kent CT11 9DS
0843–595522

Scandinavian Seaways
Parkeston Quay
Harwich, Essex CO12 4QG
0255–240240

Sealink Stena Line
Charter House
Park Street
Ashford, Kent TN24 8EX
0233–647047

TRAVELLING ABROAD BY TRAIN

Rail Travel in Europe

British Rail International
Hudson's Place
Victoria
London SW1V 1JY
071–834 2345

Austria

Contact individual stations for assistance.

Belgium

Belgian National Railways
Premier House
10 Greycoat Place
London SW1P 1SB
071–233 0360

Denmark

DSB (Danish Railways)
c/o Scandinavian Seaways
Parkeston Quay
Harwich, Essex CO12 4QG
0255–240240

Finland

Finlandia Travel Agency Ltd
223 Regent Street
London W1R 7DB
071–409 7334/7335

France

French Railways (SNCF)
179 Piccadilly
London W1V 0BA
071–409 3518

OR

SNCF English Language Information Service
From the UK: 010–33-1 45 820841

Germany *

German Rail Sales (for booklet)
DER Travel Service
18 Conduit Street
London W1R 9TD
071–499 0577

Italy

CIT
50 Conduit Street
London W1R 9FB
071–434 3844

Ireland

Irish Rail Travel Centre
Abbey Street
Dublin 1, Eire
010–35–31 366222

Luxembourg

Luxembourg National Railways
Place de la Gare
Luxembourg

Netherlands *

(Information and assistance)
From the UK: 010–31–30 355555

Netherlands Railways
25–28 Buckingham Gate
London SW1E 6LD
071–630 1735

---

* Information booklet available (French and Swiss booklets not in English)

TRAVELLING ABROAD

Norway

Norwegian State Railways
21–24 Cockspur Street
London SW1Y 5DA
071–930 6666

Portugal

Portuguese National Tourist Office
New Bond Street House
1–5 New Bond Street
London W1Y 0NP
071–494 1441

Spain

Spanish National Tourist Office
57–58 St. James Street
London SW1A 1LD
071–499 0901

Sweden

NSR Travel Bureau
21–24 Cockspur Street
London SW1Y 5DA
071–930 6666

Switzerland *

Swiss National Tourist Office
Swiss Centre
1 New Coventry Street
London W1V 8EE
071–734 1921

TRAVELLING ABROAD BY AIR

Air Travel

Access To The Skies Committee
c/o RADAR
25 Mortimer Street
London W1N 8AB
071–637 5400

Air Transport Users' Committee
2nd Floor, Kingsway House
103 Kingsway
London WC2B 6QX
071–242 3882

British Airways Invalid Passenger Unit
The Queen's Building Health Centre
Heathrow Airport
Hounslow, Middlesex TW6 2JA
081–562 7070

British Rail (BR)
Area Manager
Victoria Station
London SW1 1JU
071–922 6215
(For Assistance: Victoria to Gatwick)

Civil Aviation Authority (CAA)
Greville House
37 Gratton Road
Cheltenham, Glos. GL50 2BN
0242–235151

Disabled Living Foundation (DLF)
380–384 Harrow Road
London W9 2HU
071–289 6111

Gatwick Airport Ltd
Gatwick Airport, W. Sussex RH6 0NP
0293–567675

Gatwick Airport
Main Car Park Office
0293–502896

Gatwick Travel Care
Room 3058, Gatwick Village
Gatwick Airport, W. Sussex RH6 0NP
0293–504283

Guide Dogs for the Blind Association
Hillfield, Burghfield Common
Reading, Berkshire RG7 3YG
0734–835555

---

* Information booklet available (French and Swiss booklets not in English)

Heathrow Airport Ltd
Heathrow Airport
Hounslow, Middlesex TW6 1JH
     Terminal 1: 081–745 7702/4
       Terminal 2: 081–745 7115/7
       Terminal 3: 081–745 7412/4
       Terminal 4: 081–745 4540

Heathrow Airport
Short-stay Car Park Office
081–745 7623

Heathrow Airport
Long-stay Car Park Office
081–745 7973

Heathrow Travel Care
Room 1214, Queen's Building
Heathrow Airport
Hounslow, Middlesex TW6 1JH
081–745 7495

International Air Transport Association
  (IATA)
Public Information Department
Imperial House
15–19 Kingsway
London WC2B 6UN
071–240 9036

London City Airport
King George V Dock
Silvertown
London E16 2PX
071–474 5555

London Transport
Unit For Disabled Passengers
55 Broadway
London SW1H OBD
071–222 5600

Luton Airport Ltd
Luton, Beds. LU2 7LY
0582–405100

Royal National Institute for the Blind (RNIB)
224 Great Portland Street
London W1N 6AA
071–388 1266

Spinal Injuries Association (SIA)
76 St. James's Lane
London N10 3DF
081–444 2121

Stansted Airport Ltd
Stansted
Essex CM24 8QW
0279–502380

8. HOLIDAYS

▶ TYPES OF HOLIDAY

There is a wide variety of holidays available now to people with disabilities. They fall into two main groups:

- Holidays for everyone, but which offer special travel and accommodation facilities for disabled people who need them.

- Holidays with full accommodation and care facilities specially designed for disabled people.

Holidays in both categories can be found both at home and abroad. In 1990 the Tourism For All campaign was launched by the British Tourist Authority (BTA) in conjunction with Holiday Care Service to encourage all elements of the British tourism industry to meet the needs of disabled people who have special requirements.

If you are going on holiday in the UK, you should see Chapter 5 "Travelling Further Afield" for information and contacts which may help you in getting to your holiday destination.

The Disabled Travel Information Centre is a voluntary organisation with information on travel, transport and holidays in the UK and abroad. They organise day trips and have access to their own transport. Membership may give concessions on cross-Channel ferries.

HOLIDAYS

► HOLIDAYS ABROAD

Many tour operators now make arrangements for disabled people in their package tours and there are companies which specially cater for disabled people, some offering 'special interest' holidays.

If you are travelling abroad on holiday by car, sea, rail or air you should have a look at Chapter 7 "Travelling Abroad" for information and contacts which may be of help. If you are going on a package holiday do check with your travel agent that the travel arrangements will be satisfactory for you.

► COACH HOLIDAYS

Some companies organise coach tours in the UK and abroad with fully (w) accessible luxury coaches (some also supply helpers). These tours can be joined by individual disabled people or groups. Full details of these companies can be found in "Holidays in the British Isles: A Guide for Disabled People" or "Holidays and Travel Abroad: A Guide for Disabled People" published by the Royal Association for Disability and Rehabilitation (RADAR) and available from their office, or from branches of WH Smith. You can also get information about these holidays from Holiday Care Service.

There are also bus and coach operators who have adapted vehicles for hire to voluntary organisations and associations of disabled people. These can carry wheelchair users and ambulant disabled people as well as their escorts. Information about these companies can be obtained from the Bus and Coach Council (which also publishes a free booklet, "Getting Around By Bus and Coach: A Guide For People With Disabilities").

Two organisations run coach holidays abroad, particularly for more severely disabled people, which are fully staffed with helpers, some of whom are medically qualified:

The Across Trust

The Jumbo Ambulance Project

► CRUISES

Most cruise ships have limited facilities on board to enable disabled people to enjoy cruise holidays, and an increasing number are providing a greater range of facilities for the disabled traveller. When booking a cruise holiday you must tell the cruise operator what your disability is, and whether you need to use a wheelchair. Some cruise lines require some form of medical clearance before accepting a booking.

Wheelchair Users

If you need to use a wheelchair, most cruise lines will insist on your being accompanied by an able-bodied companion. Some ships are more suitable than others and you should check whether the toilets and/or bathrooms are (w) accessible and whether there are sills at the doorways which make access difficult.

Page and Moy Ltd, in consultation with RADAR, have produced a free guide, "Cruising And The Disabled Traveller" which gives a summary of facilities to help disabled passengers on the ships of different cruise lines. Page and Moy can provide detailed information on these facilities and can answer any question you have on cruises for people with disabilities. They can also handle your booking for you.

▶ HELP AVAILABLE WITH HOLIDAYS

There are many organisations which can give you the help you need, both in planning a holiday and whilst you are on holiday. Holiday Care Service is a registered charity which offers free information on a wide range of holidays and on all aspects of taking a holiday. They can also supply free information sheets.

Some disability organisations offer special help to their own members in taking a holiday. For a list of major national disability organisations see Appendix A.

- There are organisations which have (w) accessible self-catering accommodation available.

- Some disability associations or trusts operate holiday centres specially designed, and with care provided, for disabled people.

- Many disability organisations have their own holiday homes (self-catering or hotel type) for members.

Information about all of these can be obtained from Holiday Care Service, your own disability organisation, or the RADAR holiday guides.

If You Are Deaf Or Hard Of Hearing

The British Deaf Association can give you information about their holidays for people who are deaf or hard of hearing.

If You Are Blind Or Partially Sighted

The Royal National Institute For The Blind (RNIB) has holiday hotels and homes available with special facilities for people who are blind or partially sighted.

▶ CONCESSIONS AND FUNDING

You should see Chapter 5 "Travelling Further Afield" and Chapter 7 "Travelling Abroad" for travel concessions which are generally available. Page and Moy Ltd offer concessions on cruises booked through them.

Help in meeting the cost of a holiday can sometimes be provided by one of the organisations in the following groups:

- disability organisations
- age-related charities
- trade or professional organisations
- religious organisations
- local charities

Details and lists can be supplied by Holiday Care Service and RADAR.

HOLIDAYS

Statutory Holiday Provision

Under Section 2 of The Chronically Sick and Disabled Persons Act 1970 any disabled person, or any family with a member who is disabled, is entitled to *apply* to their local Social Services Department (Social Work Department in Scotland) to take part in any holiday organised by the Department or to receive financial assistance in making independent holiday arrangements. To be successful you will have to meet a number of conditions, and funding is limited. You should contact your local Social Services Department (Social Work Department in Scotland) for further information.

Remember

- You can take holidays with all the facilities you need, without having to be part of a group of disabled people.

- If you need special care, holidays can be arranged with care provided, both in the UK and abroad.

- Always check with your tour operator or travel agent the availability of the facilities you will need *before* you book.

- If you are travelling abroad and you are taking medication, make sure you take enough supplies with you; medical supplies can cost much more in other countries, especially the U.S.A.

▶ USEFUL CONTACTS

Association of British Travel Agents (ABTA)
Public Affairs Department
55–57 Newman Street
London W1P 4AH
071–637 2444

Across Trust
70–72 Bridge Road
East Molesey, Surrey
081–783 1355

British Deaf Association
38 Victoria Place
Carlisle, Cumbria CA1 1HU
0228–48844 (Voice)
0228–28719 (Vistel)

British Tourist Authority (BTA)
Thames Tower
Black's Road
London W6 9EL
081–846 9000

Bus and Coach Council
Sardinia House
52 Lincoln's Inn Fields
London WC2A 3LZ
071–831 7546

Disabled Travel Information Centre
346 Hawthorne Crescent
Cosham
Portsmouth, Hants. PO6 2TU
0705–324925 (Peggy Higginbottom)

Holiday Care Service
2 Old Bank Chambers
Station Road
Horley, Surrey RH6 9UY
0293–77455

The Jumbo Ambulance Project
394 Shields Road
Newcastle Upon Tyne
Tyne and Wear NE6 2YG
091–224 0030

Page and Moy Ltd
PO Box 155
Leicester LE1 9GZ
0533–513377

Royal Association For Disability And
    Rehabilitation (RADAR)
25 Mortimer Street
London W1N 8AB
071–637 5400

Royal National Institute For The Blind
    (RNIB)
224 Great Portland Street
London W1N 6AA
071–388 1266

TRIPSCOPE
63 Esmond Road
London W4 1JE
081–994 9294 (Minicom available)

AND

Pamwell House
160 Pennywell Road
Bristol BS5 0TX
0272–414094

APPENDIX A

▶ **GEOGRAPHICAL DIRECTORY**

ENGLAND

Major National Disability and Voluntary Organisations

Age Concern England
1268 London Road
Norbury, Croydon SW16 4ER
081–679 8000

Alzheimers Disease Society
158–160 Balham High Road
London SW12 9BN
081–675 6557

Arthritis Care
18 Stevenson Way
London NW1 2HD
071–916 1500

Association for Spina Bifida and
  Hydrocephalus (ASBAH)
ASBAH House
42 Park Road
Peterborough PE1 2UQ
0733–555988

Association to Combat Huntingtons Chorea
108 Battersea High Street
London SW11 3HP
071–223 7000

British Association of Cancer United
  Patients (BACUP)
121–123 Charterhouse Street
London EC1M 6AA
071–608 1661
  (freephone for callers outside London:
  0800–181199; one-to-one counselling:
  071–608 1038)

British Association of the Hard of Hearing
7–11 Armstrong Road
London W3 7JL
081–743 1110 (voice & minicom)

British Council of Organisations of Disabled
  People (BCODP)
De Bradelei House
Chapel Street
Belper, Derbyshire DE5 1AR
0773–828182

British Deaf Association
38 Victoria Place
Carlisle CA1 1HU
0228–48844 (minicom: 0228–28719)

British Epilepsy Association
Anstey House
40 Hanover Square
Leeds LS3 1BE
0532–439393

British Heart Foundation
14 Fitzharding Street
London W1H 4DH
071–935 0158

British Limbless Ex-Servicemen's
  Association (BLESMA)
Frankland Moore House
185–187 High Road
Chadwell Heath, Essex RM6 6NA
081–590 1124

British Lung Foundation
8 Peterborough Mews
London SW6 3NL
071–371 7704

British Polio Fellowship
Bell Close
West End Road
Ruislip, Middlesex HA4 6LP
0895–675515

British Red Cross Society
National Headquarters
9 Grosvenor Crescent
London SW1X 7EJ
071–235 5454

British Sports Association for the Disabled
(BSAD)
Soulcast House
13–27 Brunswick Place
London N1 6DX
071–490 4919

Centre for Accessible Environment
35 Great Smith Street
London SW1P 3BJ
071–222 7980

DIAL UK
Park Lodge
St. Catherine's Hospital
Tickhill Road
Balby, Doncaster, S. Yorks. DN4 8QN
0302–310123

Disability Alliance (ERA)
Universal House
88–94 Wentworth Street
London E1 7SA
071–247 8776

Disabled Income Group (DIG)
Millmead Business Centre
Millmead Road
London N17 9QU
081–801 8013

Friedrichs Ataxia Group
Copse Edge
Thursley Road
Elstead
Godalming, Surrey GU8 6DJ
0252–702864

Guide Dogs for the Blind Association
(GDBA)
Hillfields
Burghfield Common
Reading, Berks. RG7 3YG
0734–835555

Help the Aged
St. James' Walk
London EC1R 0BE
071–253 0253

Holiday Care Service
2 Old Bank Chambers
Station Road
Horley, Surrey RH6 9HW
0293–774535

John Grooms Association for Disabled
People
10 Gloucester Drive
Finsbury Park
London N4 2LP
081–802 7272

Multiple Sclerosis Society of Great Britain &
Northern Ireland
25 Effie Road
London SW6 1EE
071–736 6267

Muscular Dystrophy Group of Great Britain
& Northern Ireland
7–11 Prescott Place
London SW4 6BS
071–720 8055

National Association of Citizens Advice
Bureaux
Myddleton House
115–123 Pentonville Road
London N1 9LZ
071–833 2181

National Association for Mental Health
(MIND)
22 Harley Street
London W1N 2ED
071–637 0741

National Council for Voluntary
   Organisations (NCVO)
Regent's Wharf
8 All Saints Street
London N1 9RL
071–713 6161

National Association for Limbless Disabled
31 The Mall
Ealing, London W5 2PX
081–579 1758/9

National Deaf Blind League
18 Rainbow Court
Paston Ridings
Peterborough PE4 6UP
0733–573511

National Deaf-Blind and Rubella
   Association (SENSE)
311 Grays Inn Road
London WC1X 8PT
071–278 1005

National Federation of the Blind
Unity House
Westgate
Wakefield, W. Yorks. WF1 1ER
0924–291313

Parkinsons Disease Society of the UK
22 Upper Woburn Place
London WC1H 0RA
071–383 3513

PHAB, Physically Handicapped & Able
   Bodied
14 London Road
Croydon CRO 2TA
081–667 9443

Queen Elizabeth Foundation for the
   Disabled
Leatherhead Court
Woodlands Road
Leatherhead, Surrey KT22 0BN
0372–822204

Royal Association for Disability and
   Rehabilitation (RADAR)
25 Mortimer Street
London W1N 8AB
071–637 5400

Royal National Institute for the Blind
   (RNIB)
224 Great Portland Street
London W1N 6AA
071–388 1266

Royal National Institute for Deaf People
   (RNID)
105 Gower Street
London WC1E 6AH
071–387 8033 (Voice & minicom)

Royal Society for Mentally Handicapped
   Children and Adults (MENCAP)
123 Golden Lane
London EC1Y 0RT
071–454 0454

St. John Ambulance Association
HQ St. John Ambulance
1 Grosvenor Crescent
London SW1X 7EF
071–235 5231

SKILL (National Bureau for Students with
   Disabilities)
336 Brixton Road
London SW9 7AA
071–274 0565

Spinal Injuries Association
Newpoint House
76 St. James Lane
London N10 3DF
081–444 2121

Spastics Society
12 Park Crescent
London W1N 4EQ
071–636 5020
       Helpline: 0800–626216

Thalidomide Society UK
Southville
Water End Road
Potten End
Berkhamstead, Herts.
0442–872875

Womens Royal Voluntary Service
Headquarters
234–244 Stockwell Road
London SW9 9SP
071–416 0146

▶ METROPOLITAN DISTRICT COUNCILS

Greater Manchester

Social Services Departments

City of Manchester
PO Box 536
Town Hall Extension
Manchester M60 2AF
061–234 5000

Bolton Metropolitan Borough Council
Civic Centre
Le Mans Crescent
Bolton BL1 1SE
0204–22311

Metropolitan Borough of Bury
Craighouse
Bank Street
Bury BL9 ODN
061–705 5000

Oldham Metropolitan Borough
Level 13, Civic Centre
West Street
Oldham OL1 1UN
061–624 0505

Rochdale Metropolitan Borough Council
Municipal Offices
Smith Street
Rochdale OL16 1XG
0706–47474

Salford City Council
Crompton House
100 Chorley Road
Swinton M27 2BP
061–794 4711

Metropolitan Borough of Stockport
Ponsonby House
Edward Street
Stockport SK1 3XE
061–480 4949

Tameside Metropolitan Borough
Wellington Road
Ashton-under-Lyne OL6 6DL
061–330 8355

Trafford Metropolitan Borough Council
PO Box 16, Warbrick House
35–37 Washway Road
Sale M33 1DJ
061–872 2101

Wigan Metropolitan Borough Council
Civic Centre
Millgate
Wigan WN1 1XD
0942–44991

Useful Contacts

Bury & District Disabled Advisory Council
Herbert Coates Community Centre
Morely Street
Bury BL9 9JQ
061–797 4898

DIAL Oldham
New Vale House
Greaves Street
Oldham, Greater Manchester 0L1 1DW
061–628 2271

Greater Manchester Passenger Transport
Executive
PO Box 429, Magnum House
9 Portland Street
Manchester M60 1HX
061–228 6400

Greater Manchester Regional Centre for
Disabled Living
Disabled Living Services
Redbank House
4 St Chad Street
Cheetham, Manchester M8 8QA
061–832 3678

DIAL Salford & Bolton
Guild Hall
Guild Avenue
Walkden, Worsley M28 5AS
061–799 2222

DIAL Tameside
Festival Hall
Peel Street
Denton M34 3JM
061–320 8333

DIAL Trafford
Crossford
Highfield Close
Stretford M32 8NE
061–864 2262

DIAL Wigan
Larch Avenue Day Centre
Larch Avenue
Wigan WN5 9QN
0942–215219

Oldham Advice Service for the
Handicapped & Disabled
Oldham Citizens Advice Bureau
24 Clegg Street
Oldham OL1 1PL
061–633 4350

Stockport Disability Group
Bamford Close
31a Adswood Lane West
Cale Green, Stockport SK3 8HT
061–480 7248

Tameside Association of Handicapped &
Disabled
3 Wellington Place
Dukinfield, Manchester SK16 4LE
061–339 0708

Trafford Disabled People's Forum
Trafford Metropolitan Borough Council
Social Services Department
PO Box 16, Warbrick House
35–37 Washway Road
Sale M33 1DJ
061–872 2101

Merseyside

Social Services Departments:

Metropolitan Borough of Knowsley
Municipal Buildings
Archway Road
Huyton, Liverpool L36 9UX
051–489 6000

Liverpool City Council
26 Hatton Garden
Liverpool L3 2AW
051–227 3911

Metropolitan Borough of St Helens
Century House
Hardshaw Street
St Helens WA10 1RN
0744–24061

Metropolitan Borough of Sefton
2nd Floor, Burlington House
Crosby Road North
Merseyside L22 OPF
051–922 4040

Metropolitan Borough of Wirral
Social Services Centre
Cleveland Street
Birkenhead L41 6BL
051–647 7000

GEOGRAPHICAL DIRECTORY

Useful Contacts

Merseyside Passenger Transport Executive
(MERSEYTRAVEL)
24 Hatton Garden
Liverpool L3 2AN
051–227 5181

Wirral Association for Disability
Room 38, Social Services Centre
Cleveland Street
Birkenhead, Merseyside L41 6BL
051–647 6162

South Yorkshire

Social Services Departments:

Barnsley Metropolitan Borough Council
Regent House
11 Regent Street
Barnsley S70 2DU
0226–770770

Doncaster Metropolitan Borough Council
Frenchgate Centre
24 St Sepulchre Gate
Doncaster DN1 1PH
0302–734444

Rotherham Metropolitan Borough Council
Crinoline House
Effingham Square
Rotherham S65 1DB
0709–382121

Sheffield City Council
Redvers House
Union Street
Sheffield S1 2JQ
0742–734811

Useful Contacts

DIAL Barnsley
Moorland Avenue Social Centre
Moorland Avenue
Barnsley S70 6PH
0226–240273

DIAL Rotherham
Brian O'Malley Library
Walker Place
Rotherham S65 1JH
0709–373658

DIAL Sheffield
100 Park Grange Road
Sheffield S2 3RA
0742–727996

Doncaster & District Association for the
   Welfare of the Disabled
28 Christchurch Road
Doncaster DN1 2QL
0302–349098

Rotherham & District Association for the
   Disabled
Social Centre
Oakdale Road
Holmes, Rotherham S61 2NU
0709–563253

Sheffield & District Association for the
   Disabled
751–753 Eccleshall Road
Sheffield S11 8TH
0742–660673

South Yorkshire Passenger Transport
   Executive
Exchange Street
Sheffield S2 5SZ
0742–767575

Tramline
0742–768688

Tyne & Wear

Social Services Departments :

Gateshead Metropolitan Borough Council
Civic Centre
Regent Street
Gateshead NE8 1HH
091–477 1011

Newcastle upon Tyne City Council
Civic Centre
Newcastle upon Tyne NE1 8PA
091–232 8520

North Tyneside Metropolitan Borough
  Council
Citadel East
Killingworth,
Newcastle upon Tyne NE12 0RS
091–257 5544

South Tyneside Metropolitan Borough
  Council
South Tyneside House
Westoe Road
South Shields NE33 2RL
091–427 1717

Borough of Sunderland
Town Hall & Civic Centre
Burdon Road
Sunderland SR2 7DN
091–567 6161

Useful Contacts

Gateshead Council on Disability
John Haswell House
8–9 Gladstone Terrace
Gateshead NE8 4DY
091–477 3558

Newcastle upon Tyne Council for the
  Disabled
The Dene Centre
Castle Farm Road
Gosforth, Newcastle upon Tyne NE3 1PH
091–284 0480

Tyne & Wear Passenger Transport Executive
Cuthbert House
All Saints
Newcastle upon Tyne NE1 2DA
091–261 0431

Tyne & Wear Passenger Transport Executive
TRAVELINE (Travel Information Only)
091–232 5325

West Midlands

Social Services Departments:

City of Birmingham
Snow Hill House
10–15 Livery Street
Birmingham B3 2BR
021–235 2697

Coventry City Council
Earle Street
Coventry CV1 5RR
0203–833333

Dudley Metropolitan Borough Council
Ednam House
St James Road
Dudley DY1 3JJ
0384–456000

Sandwell Metropolitan Borough Council
12 Lombard Street
West Bromwich, Sandwell B70 8RT
021–569 2200

Solihull Metropolitan Borough Council
PO Box 32, Council House
Solihull B91 3QY
021–704 6000

Walsall Metropolitan Borough Council
Civic Centre
Darwall Street
Walsall WS1 1RG
0922–650000

Wolverhampton Borough Council
Civic Centre
St Peter's Square
Wolverhampton WV1 1RT
0902–27811

Useful Contacts

DIAL Sandwell
The Carers Centre
Edward Cheshire House
2 Bearwood Road
Smethwick B66 4HH
021–558 7003

Chelmsley Wood Fellowship of the
  Handicapped
78 Heathmere Drive
Fordbridge, Birmingham B37 5EU
021–770 6277

Coventry Council for the Disabled
26A Starley Road
Coventry CV1 3JU
0203–226006

Darlaston Fellowship of the Disabled
2 Windgate Road
Bentley, Walsall WS2 0AS
0922–32132

DIAL Coventry
26A Starley Road
Coventry CV1 3JU
0203–226747 or 0203–226006

DIAL Solihull
Lowbank Day Centre
Chichester Avenue
Chelmsley Wood, Solihull B37 5RZ
021–770 0333

Solihull Society for the Physically
  Handicapped
23 White House Way
Solihull B97 1SG
021–705 5533

West Midlands Council for Disabled People
Moseley Hall Hospital
Alcester Road
Moseley, Birmingham B13 8JL
021–449 1225

Centro
(West Midlands Passenger Transport
  Executive)
Commercial Department
16 Summer Lane
Birmingham B19 3SD
021–206 2700

Hotline Birmingham 021–200 2700
Hotline Coventry 0203–555211

West Yorkshire

Social Services Departments:

City of Bradford Metropolitan Council
Olicana House
Chapel Street
Bradford BD1 5RE
0274–752111

Metropolitan Borough of Calderdale
Wellesley Park
Gilbert Street
Halifax HX2 0BA
0422–363561

Kirklees Metropolitan Borough Council
Oldgate House
2 Oldgate
Huddersfield HD1 6QF
0484–422133

Leeds City Council
Select A Post 9
Sweet Street
Leeds LS11 9DQ
0532–478630

Wakefield City Metropolitan District
  Council
87 Northgate
Wakefield WF1 3DA
0924–290900

Useful Contacts

Calderdale Disabled Advice Resource Team
  (DART)
DIAL
36 Gibbet Street
Halifax HX1 5BA
0422–346950 or 0422–346040

DIAL Bradford
103 Dockfield Road
Shipley BD17 7AP
0274–594173

DIAL Kirklees
Huddersfield Day Centre
Zetland Street
Huddersfield HD1 2RA
0484–45300 ext.228/230

DIAL Leeds
The William Merritt Centre
St Mary's Hospital
Greenhill Road
Armley LS12 3QE
0532–795583

DIAL Wakefield
33 Dewsbury Road
Wakefield WF2 9BL
0924–379181

Kirklees (North) Disability Services
Dewsbury Day Centre
Town Hall Way
Dewsbury, West Yorkshire WF12 8EQ
0924–455149

West Yorkshire Passenger Transport
    Executive
Wellington House
40–50 Wellington Street
Leeds LS1 2DE
0232–440988

▶ ENGLISH COUNTIES

Avon

Department of Social Services
Avon County Council
PO Box 30
Avon House North
St James Barton
Bristol BS99 7NB
0272–290777

Public Transport Coordination
County Engineer and Surveyor's
    Department
Avon County Council
PO Box 87, Avon House North
St James Barton
Bristol BS99 7SG
0272–290777

Useful Contacts

DIAL Bristol
(Disability Advice Centre)
Pamwell House
160 Pennywell Road
Bristol BS5 0TX
0272–413008

DIAL
Weston-Super-Mare
Room 5, Roselawn
28 Walliscote Road
Weston-Super-Mare BS23 1UJ
0934–419 426 (Tues. & Thurs. 2–4 pm)

Bath Association for the Disabled
1 Cleveland Cottages
Walcot
Bath, Avon BA1 5DD
0225–332646

Begbrook & Stapleton Disabled Community
    Council
30 Nuthatch Gardens
Bristol BS16 1JF
0272–652104

Bristol Council for Disabled Adults
75 Whiteladies Road
Bristol BS8 2NT
0272–734007

Disability Advice Centre
1st Floor, Canningford House
38 Victoria Street
Bristol BS1 6BY
0272–273367

Kingswood Council for the Disabled
c/o Kingswood Borough Council
Civic Centre
High Street
Kingswood, Bristol BS15 2TR
0272–601121 ext.380

Nailsea Disabled Club
4 Sir John's Wood
Bristol BS19 1DX
0275–854889

GEOGRAPHICAL DIRECTORY

Bedfordshire

Department of Social Services
Bedfordshire County Council
County Hall
Cauldwell Street
Bedford, Beds. MK42 9AP
0234–363222

Passenger Transport Officer
Department of Transportation &
 Engineering
Bedfordshire County Council
County Hall
Bedford, Beds. MK42 9AP
0234–363222

Useful Contacts

DIAL Bedfordshire
101 Dallow Road
Luton, Beds. LU1 1NW
0582–400461 (Mon.-Fri. 09.30–12.30)

Berkshire

Department of Social Services
Berkshire County Council
Shire Hall
Shinfield Park
Reading, Berks. RG2 9XH
0734–875444

Public Transport Coordinator
Policy Unit, Highways & Planning
 Department
Berkshire County Council
Shire Hall
Shinfield Park
Reading, Berks. RG2 9XG
0734–875444

Useful Contacts

DIAL Berkshire
Acorn Centre
78 Bath Road
Reading RG3 2BE
0734–505900 (Tues. & Thurs. 3.30–7.30)

Red Cross Disabled Club
134 Springfield Road
Windsor, Berks. SL4 3PU
0753–865444

Buckinghamshire

Department of Social Services
Buckinghamshire County Council
Old County Hall
Walton Street
Aylesbury, Bucks. HP20 1EZ
0296–395000

Passenger Transport Section
County Engineer's Department
Buckinghamshire County Council
County Hall
Aylesbury, Bucks. HP20 1YZ
0296–382000

Busline Enquiry Number (any bus in or
 through Bucks.)
0296–382000 (Mon.-Fri.9–5)

Useful Contacts

DIAL Buckinghamshire
c/o Occupational Therapy Department
Milton Keynes Hospital
Standing Way
Eaglestone, Milton Keynes MK6 5AZ
0908–660033 ext. 2509 (Mon. & Wed. 10–4)

DIAL High Wycombe
Desborough Road Family Centre
Richardson Street
High Wycombe, Bucks. HP11 2SB
0494–442601 (Mon. 2–4, Wed. 10–12 & 2–4,
 Fri. 10–12)

Milton Keynes Council of Disabled People
c/o Oliver Wells School
Farnborough, Netherfield
Milton Keynes, Bucks. MK4 4HG
0908–677415

Cambridgeshire

Department of Social Services
Cambridgeshire County Council
Castle Court, Shire Hall
Castle Hill, Cambridge CB3 0AP
0223–317744

Transport Coordinating Officer
Transportation Department
Cambridgeshire County Council
Castle Court, Shire Hall
Cambridge CB3 0AP
0223–317744

Useful Contacts

DIAL Peterborough
Kingfisher Centre
The Cresset
Bretton, Peterborough PE3 8DX
0733–265551 (Mon. Tues. Thurs. Fri. 10–4)

Kingfisher Centre
The Cresset
Bretton, Peterborough PE3 8DX
0733–260699

Fenland Association for the Disabled
Manfield, Back Road
Gorefield, Wisbech PE13 4NW
0945–870539

Peterborough Council for the Disabled
c/o Mr M Moore
9 Peterborough Road
Eye, Peterborough PE6 7YA
0733–222291

Cheshire

Department of Social Services
Cheshire County Council
Commerce House
Hunter Street
Chester CH1 2QP
0244–602424

County Transport Coordinator
Department of Highways & Transportation
Cheshire County Council
Backford Hall
Chester CH1 6QA
0244–603634

Useful Contacts

Chester & District Committee for Disabled
    People
Dial House
Hamilton Place
Chester CH1 2BH
0244–345655

DIAL Cheshire
Dial House
Hamilton Place
Chester CH1 2BH
0244–345655

Cleveland

Department of Social Services
Cleveland County Council
Marton House
Borough Road
Middlesbrough TS4 2EH
0642–248155

Group Engineer (Transport Coordination)
County Surveyor's & Engineer's
    Department
Cleveland County Council
PO Box 77, Gurney House
Gurney Street
Middlesbrough TS1 1JL
0642–248155

Useful Contacts

Alma Street Centre for the Disabled
Alma Street
Stockton-on-Tees
Cleveland
0642–601580

GEOGRAPHICAL DIRECTORY

Billingham Physically Handicapped Club
Everard Ellis Centre
Mill Lane
Billingham
0642–552583

Cleveland Spastics Work & Welfare Centre
Acklam Road, nr West Lane Hospital
Middlesbrough TS5 4EG
0642–818854

DIAL Middlesbrough
Middlesbrough General Hospital
Ayresome Green Lane
Middlesbrough TS5 5AZ
0642–827471

Cornwall

Department of Social Services
Cornwall County Council
Old County Hall
Station Road
Truro TR1 3AU
0872–74282

Social Services Transport Officer
Chief Executive to Clerks Department
Cornwall County Council
County Hall
Treyew Road
Truro TR1 3AY
0872–74282

Useful Contacts

Cornwall Disabled Association
56 Lemon Street
Truro TR1 2PE
0872–73518

Saltash Handicapped & Disabled
   Organisation
SHADO Centre
Callington Road
Saltash, Cornwall
0752–848780

Cumbria

Department of Social Services
Cumbria County Council
37 Victoria Place
Carlisle, Cumbria CA1 1EJ
0228–23456

Public Transport Officer
Department of Highways & Transportation
Cumbria County Council
Citadel Chambers
Citadel Row, Carlisle CA3 8SG
0228–23456

Useful Contacts

Allerdale Association for the Disabled
(and DIAL Allerdale)
39 Brow Top
Workington, Cumbria CA14 5DP
0900–65555

Barrow & District Council for the Disabled
73–75 School Street
Barrow in Furness, Cumbria LA14 1DR
0229–833553

DIAL Barrow
73–75 School Street
Barrow in Furness
Cumbria LA14 1DR
0229–833553

DIAL South Lakeland
102 Highgate
Kendal, Cumbria LA9 4HE
0539–740508

DIAL Workington
39 Brow Top
Workington CA14 5DP
0900–65555

Derbyshire

Department of Social Services
Derbyshire County Council
County Offices
Matlock, Derbyshire DE4 3AG
0629–580000

Head of Public Transport
Public Transport Unit, Derbyshire County
    Council
Chatsworth Hall, Chesterfield Road
Matlock DE4 3FW
0269–580000

Useful Contacts

Derby Centre for Integrated Living
Long Close, Cemetery Lane
Derby DE5 3HY
0773–740246

Derbyshire Association for the Disabled
46 Bamsfield
Hawk Green
Marple, Cheshire SK6 7JB
061–427 5944

Derby Coalition of Disabled People
Victoria Buildings
117 High Street
Clay Cross, Chesterfield S45 9DZ
0246–865305

Devon

Department of Social Services
Devon County Council
County Hall
Topsham Road, Exeter EX2 4QR
0392–382331

Public Transport Advisor
Transport Coordination Centre
Engineering & Planning Department
County Hall, Topsham Road
Exeter EX2 4QR
0392–382123

Useful Contacts

Devon Association of Disabled Fellowships
3 Woolsery Grove
Whipton, Exeter EX4 8BL
0392–68627

DIAL Exeter
Ashclyst Centre
Old Whipton Hospital
Hospital Lane
Whipton, Exeter EX1 3RB
0392–64205

DIAL Honiton & District
Honiton Advice & Information Centre
48–50 New Street
Honiton EX14 8BS
0404–41212

DIAL Plymouth
Plymouth Guild of Community Service
Ernest English House
Buckwell Street, Plymouth PL1 2DA
0752–665084

Dorset

Department of Social Services
Dorset County Council
County Hall
Dorchester DT1 1XJ
0305–251000

Group Leader, Public Transport
County Surveyor's Department
Dorset County Council
County Hall
Dorchester DT1 1XJ
0305–251000

Useful Contacts

DIAL Dorset
Dial House
76 Lagland Street
Poole BH15 1QG
0202–677559

Dorset Association for the Disabled
Weymouth Outdoor Education Centre
Knightsdale Road
Weymouth DT4 0HS
0305–761840

Healthpoint
Poole General Library, Dolphin Centre
Poole, Dorset BH15 1QE
0202–675377

OR

Help for Health
Highcroft Cottage
Romsey Road
Winchester, Hants. SO22 5DH
0962–849100

Durham

Department of Social Services
Durham County Council
County Hall
Durham DH1 5UQ
091–386 4411

Group Manager, Public Transport
Environment Department
Durham County Council
County Hall
Durham DH1 5UQ
091–386 44ll ext. 2212

Useful Contacts

Darlington Association on Disability
Friends Meeting House
6 Skinnergate
Darlington DR3 7NB
0325–461496

Durham County Association for the
    Disabled
Ground Floor Rear
Town Hall
Spennymoor, Co. Durham
0388–812288

East Sussex

Department of Social Services
East Sussex County Council
PO Box 5, County Hall
St Anne's Crescent
Lewes BN7 1SW
0273–481000

Highways & Transportation Department
East Sussex County Council
Sackville House, Brooks Close
Lewes, E. Sussex BN7 1UE
0273–481000

Useful Contacts

East Sussex Association for the Disabled
47 Western Road
Lewes, E. Sussex BN7 1XT
0273–472860

Eastbourne Association for the Disabled
8 Saffrons Road
Eastbourne BN21 1DG
0323–37369

Essex (See also London Borough of Redbridge)

Department of Social Services
Essex County Council
County Hall
Chelmsford CM1 1JZ
0245–492211

Public Transport Coordination Officer
Planning Department
Essex County Council
County Hall
Chelmsford, Essex CM1 1LF
0245–492211

Useful Contacts

DIAL Basildon
Room 7, The Basildon Centre
Pagel Mead, Basildon SS14 1DL
0265–294400

DIAL Barking & Dagenham
St Georges Day Centre
St Georges Road
Dagenham RM9 5JB
081–595 8181

DIAL Chelmsford
90 Broomfield Road
Chelmsford, Essex CM1 1SS
0245–287177

Gloucestershire

Department of Social Services
Gloucestershire County Council
Bearland Wing, Shire Hall
Gloucester GL1 2TR
0452–425100

Public Transport Manager
County Surveyor's Department
Gloucestershire County Council
Bearland Wing, Shire Hall
Gloucester GL1 2TH
0452–425609

Useful Contacts

Gloucestershire Association for the Disabled
Stuart House
Butt Street
Minchinhampton, Glos. GL6 9JS
0453–883715

Hampshire

Department of Social Services
Hampshire County Council
Trafalgar House
Trafalgar Street
Winchester SO23 9DH
0962–841841

Passenger Transport Officer
County Surveyor's Department
Hampshire County Council
The Castle
Winchester SO23 8UD
0962–846925

Useful Contacts

DIAL Hampshire
39 Prince Albert Road
Southsea, Hants. PO4 9HR
0705–824853

Havant & District Federation of the
  Handicapped
5 Mercury Place
Crookhorn, Waterlooville
Havant, Hants. PO7 8BA
0705–254510

Help for Health
Highcroft Cottage
Romsey Road
Winchester, Hants. SO22 5DH
0962–678679
OR
Healthpoint
Poole General Library, Dolphin Centre
Poole, Dorset BH15 1QE
0202–675377

Hereford & Worcester

Department of Social Services
Hereford & Worcester County Council
County Hall
Spetchley Road
Worcester WR5 2NP
0905–763763

Public Transport Coordinator
Department of Engineering & Planning
Hereford & Worcester County Council
County Hall
Spetchley Road
Worcester WR5 2NP
0905–766798

Useful Contacts

DIAL Herefordshire
15 St Owens Street
Hereford HR1 2JB
0432–277770

DIAL Worcester
23 Angel Place
Worcester WR1 3QN
0905–27790

DIAL Wyre Forest
25 Comberton Road
Kidderminster DY10 3DL
0562–68248

GEOGRAPHICAL DIRECTORY

Herefordshire Lifestyles
15 St Owens Street
Hereford HR1 2JB
0432–277968

Hertfordshire (See also London Borough of Barnet)

Department of Social Services
Hertfordshire County Council
County Hall, Pegs Lane
Hertford SG13 8DP
0992–556363

Passenger Transport Unit
Transportation Department
Trinity Centre
Fanhams Hall Road
Ware, Herts. SG12 7LU
0992–588172

Useful Contacts

Hertfordshire Association for the Disabled
The Woodside Centre
The Commons
Welwyn Garden City, Herts. AL7 4DD
0707–324581

Humberside

Department of Social Services
Humberside County Council
Flemingate House
Flemingate, Beverley HU17 ONQ
0482–871421

Principal Passenger Transport Officer
Technical Services Department
Humberside County Council
County Hall
Beverley HU17 9BA
0482–867131

Useful Contacts

DIAL Hull
Kingston Chamber
Land of Green Ginger
Hull HU1 2EA
0482–226234

Isle of Wight

Department of Social Services
Isle of Wight County Council
17 Fairlee Road
Newport, Isle of Wight PO30 1UD
0983–520600

Public Transport Officer
County Surveyor's Department
County Transport Depot
21 Whitcombe Road
Newport, Isle of Wight PO30 1YS
0983–823710

Useful Contacts

DIAL Isle of Wight
The Riverside Centre
The Quay
Newport, Isle of Wight PO32 2QR
0983–522823

Federation of Island Societies for the
    Handicapped (FISH)
48 Alexander Road
Cowes, Isle of Wight PO31 7JT
0983–298480

Kent

Department of Social Services
Kent County Council
Springfield
Maidstone, Kent ME14 2LW
0622–671411

Public Transport Planning Manager
Highways & Transportation Department
Kent County Council, Sandling Block
Springfield, Maidstone ME14 2LQ
0622–671411

Useful Contacts

DIAL Kent
The Pines
Puckle Lane
Canterbury CT1 3IA
0227–771155

DIAL North West Kent
The Bungalow
c/o The Limes
Brent Lane
Dartford DA1 1QN
0322–276714 or 0322–291362

Kent Association for the Disabled
136 Camden Road
Tunbridge Wells TN1 2QZ
0892–545211

Lancashire (see also Greater Manchester)

Department of Social Services
Lancashire County Council
PO Box 162
Eastcliff County Offices
Preston, Lancs. PR1 3EA
0772–54868

Assistant County Surveyor
Transport Coordination
County Surveyor's Department
Lancashire County Council
PO Box 9, Cross Street
Guildhouse, Preston PR1 8RD
0772–264583

Useful Contacts

DIAL West Lancashire
Skelmersdale Library
The Concourse
Skelmersdale WN8 6NL

Disability Helpline
0695–51819

Transport Enquiry Line
0282–831263

Leicestershire

Department of Social Services
Leicestershire County Council
County Hall
Glenfield, Leicester LE3 8RL
0533–323232

Busline (in and through Leicestershire)
0533–313391

Community Transport Officer
Department of Planning and Transportation
Leicestershire County Council
County Hall
Glenfield, Leicester LE3 8RJ
0533–657248

Useful Contacts

DIAL Leicestershire
76 Clarendon Park Road
Leicester LE2 3AD
0533–700666

Leicestershire Association for the Disabled
Information Service
76 Clarendon Park Road
Leicester LE2 3AD
0533–700666

Lincolnshire

Department of Social Services
Lincolnshire County Council
Wigford House, Brayford Wharf East
Lincoln LN5 7BH
0522–552222

County Transport Agency
Highways & Planning Department
Lincolnshire County Council
City Hall
Beaumont Fee, Lincoln LN1 1DN
0522–553132

Transport Hotline
0522–553135

Useful Contacts

Lincolnshire Society for the Physically
  Handicapped
Ancaster Day Centre
Boundary Street
Lincoln LN5 8NJ
0522–510759

GEOGRAPHICAL DIRECTORY

Norfolk

Department of Social Services
Norfolk County Council
County Hall
Martineau Lane
Norwich NR1 2DH
0603–611122

Public Transport Officer
County Surveyor's Department
Norfolk County Council
County Hall
Martineau Lane
Norwich NR1 2DH
0603–615722

Useful Contacts

DIAL Great Yarmouth
Compass House
Northgate Hospital
Northgate Street
Great Yarmouth, NR30 1BU
0493–857603

DIAL Norwich
38A Bull Close
Norwich NR3 1SX
0603–623543

North Yorkshire

Department of Social Services (HQ)
North Yorkshire County Council
Old Police HQ
Racecourse Lane
Northallerton DL7 8DD
0609–780780

Public Transport Officer
Highways & Transportation Department
North Yorkshire County Council
County Hall
Northallerton DL7 8AH
0609–780780

Useful Contacts

DIAL Selby & District
c/o Selby & District Day Centre
75 Brook Street
Selby YO8 0AL
0757–210495

Yorkshire Association for the Disabled
St Georges House
7–9 Harlow Oval
Harrogate, Yorkshire HG2 0AA
0423–504360 or 0423–567897

Northamptonshire

Department of Social Services
Northamptonshire County Council
Northampton House
Northampton NN1 2JE
0604–236400

Public Transport Coordinator
Planning & Transportation Department
Northamptonshire County Council
Northampton House
Northampton NN1 2HZ
0604–236712

Useful Contacts

DIAL Northamptonshire (Corby Branch)
Stonehouse, South Road
Corby NN17 1XB
0536–204742

DIAL Northamptonshire (Daventry Branch)
The Abbey Centre
Market Square
Daventry NN1
0327–704223

Northamptonshire Council for the Disabled
13 Hazlewood Road
Northampton NN1 1LG
0604–24088

Northumberland

Department of Social Services
Northumberland County Council
County Hall
Morpeth NE61 2EF
0670–514343

Public Transport Team
Northumberland County Council
County Hall
Morpeth NE61 2EF
0670–514343

Useful Contacts

Berwick Centre for Disability
10–14 Eastern Lane
Berwick upon Tweed
Northumberland TD15 1DH
0289–302908

Blyth Valley Disabled Forum
Emily Davison House
93 Bondicar Terrace
Blyth NE24 2JR
0670–364657

Nottinghamshire

Department of Social Services
Nottinghamshire County Council
County Hall
West Bridgford, Nottingham NG2 7QP
0602–823823

Public Transport Group
Planning & Economic Development
    Department
Nottinghamshire County Council
Trent Bridge House
Fox Road
West Bridgford, Nottingham NG1 6BJ
0602–823823

Useful Contacts

DIAL Mansfield & District
1 Byron Street
Mansfield NG18 5NX
0623–25891

Nottingham Resource Centre for the
    Disabled
Lenton Business Centre
Lenton Boulevard
Nottingham NG7 2BY
0602–420391

Oxfordshire

Department of Social Services
Oxfordshire County Council
Speedwell House
Speedwell Street
Oxford OX1 1UJ
0865–815538

Public Transport Officer
Department of Planning & Property Services
Oxfordshire County Council
Speedwell House
Speedwell Street
Oxford OX1 1SD
0865–815859

Useful Contacts

DIAL Oxford
Rivermead Centre
Abingdon Road
Oxford OX14 2HP
0865–791818

Shropshire

Department of Social Services
Shropshire County Council
Shire Hall, Abbey Foregate
Shrewsbury SY2 6ND
0743–253031

Public Transport Team Leader
Shropshire County Council
Shire Hall, Abbey Foregate
Shrewsbury SY2 6ND
0743–253031

Somerset

Department of Social Services
Somerset County Council
County Hall
Taunton TA1 4DY
0823–333451

Senior Assistant, Transportation
County Surveyor's Department
Somerset County Council
County Hall
Taunton TA1 4DY
0823–255695/6

Useful Contacts

DIAL Somerset
Albemarle Assembly Rooms
Albemarle Road
Taunton TA1 1BA
0823–278067

Disability Resource Centre
The Old Library
Adam Street
Burnham on Sea, Somerset TA8 1PG
0278–787477

Staffordshire

Department of Social Services
Staffordshire County Council
69 Foregate Street
Stafford ST17 2PY
0785–223121

Public Transport Coordinator
County Planning Department
Staffordshire County Council
Martin Street
Stafford ST16 2LE
0785–223121

Useful Contacts

DIAL Stoke on Trent
Trent Centre
645 Leek Road
Manley, Stoke ST1 3NF
0782–269744

Tamworth Disabled Association
27 Orchard Close
Dosthill, Tamworth B77 1NB
0827–280914

Tamworth Support & Advice for the
   Disabled
Carnegie Centre
Corporation Street
Tamworth B79 7DN
0827–66393

Suffolk

Department of Social Services
Suffolk County Council
St Paul House, County Hall
Rope Walk
Ipswich IP4 1LH
0473–230000

Public Transport Team
Highways Department
Suffolk County Council
St Edmund House, County Hall
Ipswich IP4 1LZ
0473–230000

Useful Contacts

DIAL Lowestoft & Waveney
13 Kimberley Road
Lowestoft NR33 OUV
0502–511333

DIAL MidSuffolk Rethink
c/o Family Centre
Violet Hill Road
Stowmarket IP14 1NL
0449–672781

DIAL Woodbridge
Room 1, Disablement Advice Centre
St Johns Hill
Woodbridge IP12 1HS
0394–387070 or 0394–380499

DIAL Ipswich
19 Tower Street
Ipswich IP1 3BE
0473–217313

Surrey

Department of Social Services
Surrey County Council
A.C. Court
High Street
Thames Ditton KT7 0QA
081–541 9641

Principal Public Transport Officer
Tranportation Planning Unit
Surrey County Council
County Hall
Penrhyn Road
Kingston-upon-Thames KT1 2DN
081–541 9372

Useful Contacts

DIAL Surrey
c/o Adult Education Centre
Stychen Lane
Bletchingley RH1 4LL
0883–744255

Disability Information Service
"Harrowlands", Harrowlands Park
South Terrace
Dorking RH2 2HA
0306–875156

Voluntary Association for Surrey Disabled
Victoria House
Epsom Road
Leatherhead KT22 8TA
0372–377430 or 0372–377890

Warwickshire

Department of Social Services
Warwickshire County Council
PO Box 48, Shire Hall
Warwick CV34 4RD
0926–410410

Public Transport Coordinator
Planning & Transportation Department
Barrack Street
Warwick CV34 4SX
0926–410410

Useful Contacts

DIAL Nuneaton & Bedworth
New Ramsden Centre, School Walk
Attleborough, Nuneaton CV11 4PJ
0203–349954

DIAL Rugby
20 North Street
Rugby CV21 2AG
0788–568368

West Sussex

Department of Social Services
West Sussex County Council
Grange Block
Tower Street
Chichester PO19 1QT
0243–777100

Public Transport Officer
County Surveyor's Department
West Sussex County Council
Grange Block
Tower Street
Chichester PO19 1RH
0243–777556

Useful Contacts

DIAL Mid Sussex
Room 213, Health Centre
Heath Road
Haywards Heath RH16 3AX
0444–416619

West Sussex Association for the Disabled
5 Theatre Lane
Chichester PO19 1SR
0243–774088

Wiltshire

Department of Social Services
Wiltshire County Council
County Hall
Trowbridge, Wilts. BA14 8JN
0225–753641

Public Transport Coordination
Department of Planning & Highways
Wiltshire County Council
County Hall
Trowbridge, Wilts. BA14 8JD
0225–753641 ext. 3451

Useful Contacts

DIAL Wiltshire
St Georges Hospital
St Georges Road
Semington BA14 6JQ
0380–871003

Devizes & District Association for the
Disabled
Nursteed Centre
Nursteed Road
Devizes, Wilts. SN10 5EB
0380–726420

North Wiltshire Association for the Disabled
15 Westbrook Close
Chippenham SN14 ODL
0249–651223

▶ **LONDON BOROUGHS**

Barking and Dagenham

London Borough of Barking & Dagenham
Department of Social Services
Civic Centre, Rainham Road North
Dagenham, Essex RM10 7BN
081–592 4500

Useful Contacts

Disablement Association of Barking &
Dagenham
Eileen Fairbrass Centre
Pembroke Gardens
Dagenham, Essex RM10 7YP
081–592 8603

Barnet

London Borough of Barnet
Department of Social Services
Ivy House
1331 High Road
Whetstone, Barnet N20 9HZ
081–446 1488

Useful Contacts

Disablement Association in the Borough of
Barnet
DABB Advice Centre
4 Oakleigh Gardens
Whetstone, Barnet N20 9AB
081–446 6937 (Minicom available)

Brent

London Borough of Brent
Department of Social Services
349 High Road
Wembley HA9 9AD
081–904 1244

Useful Contacts

Brent Association for Disabled People
154 Harlesden Road
Willesden NW10 3RX
081–459 1829

Bromley

London Borough of Bromley
Department of Social Services
Town Hall
Widmore Road
Bromley, Kent BR1 1SB
081–464 3333

Useful Contacts

Bromley Association for People with
Handicaps
Lewis House
30 Beckenham Road
Beckenham, Kent BR3 4LS
081–663 3345

Camden

London Borough of Camden
Department of Social Services
79 Camden Road
London NW1 9EU
071–278 4444

Useful Contacts

Disabled in Camden (DISC)
7 Crowndale Road
London NW1 1TU
071–387 0700

London Borough of Camden
Disability Unit
Room 410E, Camden Town Hall
Euston Road
London NW1 2RU
071–837 4010

City of London Corporation

City of London Corporation
Department of Social Services
Public Service Building
Milton Court, Moor Lane
London EC2Y 9BL
071–606 3030

Croydon

London Borough of Croydon
Department of Social Services
Taberner House
Park Lane
Croydon CR9 3JS
081–686 4433

Useful Contacts

Croydon Association of People with
    Disabilities (CAPD)
The Shop Front
487A Purley Way
Croydon CR0 4RG
081–760 9927

Ealing

London Borough of Ealing
Department of Social Services
26 Castlebar Road
Ealing W5 2DP
081–997 3391

Useful Contacts

Ealing Association for Disabled People
The Centre
Bayham Road
Ealing W13 0TQ
081–840 0977

Enfield

London Borough of Enfield
Department of Social Services
Civic Centre
Silver Street
Enfield EN1 3ES
081–366 6565

Useful Contacts

Enfield Disablement Association
Southgate Town Hall, Green Lanes
Palmers Green
London N13 4XD
081–447 8268

Enfield Voluntary Association for the
    Disabled
38 Gardenia Road
Bush Hill Park
Enfield EN1 2HZ
081–360 7872

Greenwich

London Borough of Greenwich
Department of Social Services
Nelson House
50 Wellington Street
Woolwich SE18 6PY
081–854 8888

Useful Contacts

Greenwich Association of Disabled People
Centre for Independent Living
Christchurch Forum
Trafalgar Road
London SE10 9EQ
081–305 2221

Hackney

London Borough of Hackney
Department of Social Services
205 Morning Lane
London E9 6JX
081–986 3123

Useful Contacts

DIAL Hackney
16 Dalston Lane
London E8 3AZ
071–275 8485

Hammersmith & Fulham

London Borough of Hammersmith and
   Fulham
Department of Social Services
145 King Street
London W6 9JU
081–748 3020

Useful Contacts

Hammersmith & Fulham Action for
   Disability (HAFAD)
The Pavilion
1 Mund Street
London W14 9LY
081–385 2156

Haringey

London Borough of Haringey
Department of Social Services
40 Cumberland Road
Wood Green, London N22 4SG
081–975 9700

Useful Contacts

Haringey Disabilities Consortium
551B High Road
Tottenham, London N17 6SB
081–801 9576

Harrow

London Borough of Harrow
Department of Social Services
Civic Centre
Station Road
Harrow HA1 2UL
081–863 5611

Useful Contacts

Harrow Association for Disability
The Lodge
64 Pinner Road
Harrow HA1 4HZ
081–427 5569

Havering

London Borough of Havering
Department of Social Services
Mercury House,
Mercury Gardens
Romford RM1 3RX
0708–766999

Useful Contacts

Havering Association for the Disabled
Whittaker Hall
1A Woodhall Crescent
Hornchurch RM11 3NN
04024–76554

Hillingdon

London Borough of Hillingdon
Department of Social Services
Civic Centre
High Street
Uxbridge UB8 1UW
0895–250111

Useful Contacts

Disablement Association Hillingdon
(DASH)
Hillingdon Independent Living Centre
Royal Lane
Uxbridge, Middlesex UB8 3QW
0895–231677

Hounslow

London Borough of Hounslow
Department of Social Services
Civic Centre
Lampton Road
Hounslow TW3 4DN
081–570 7728

Useful Contacts

Voluntary Action Centre
Hounslow Borough Association of Disabled
People (HBADP)
51 Grove Road
Hounslow TW3 3PR
081–577 3226

Islington

London Borough of Islington
Department of Social Services
Highbury House
5 Highbury Crescent
London N5 1RW
071–226 1234

Useful Contacts

DIAL Islington
Islington Advice & Rights Centre for the
Handicapped (ARCH)
90–92 Upper Street
London N1 0ND
071–359 6535

Islington Disablement Associates (IDA)
2 Upper Street
London N1 0NP
071–226 0137

Kensington & Chelsea

The Royal London Borough of Kensington
& Chelsea
Department of Social Services
The Town Hall
Hornton Street
London W8 7NX
071–937 5464

Useful Contacts

Kensington & Chelsea Action for Disability
19–27 Young Street
London W8 5EH
071–937 7073

Kingston-upon-Thames

The Royal London Borough of Kingston-
upon-Thames
Department of Social Services
Guildhall
Kingston-upon-Thames
Surrey KT1 1EU
081–546 2121

Useful Contacts

Kingston-upon-Thames Association for
Disabled People (KADP)
53 Canbury Park Road
Kingston-upon-Thames
Surrey KT2 6LQ
081–549 8893

Lambeth

London Borough of Lambeth
Department of Social Services
Mary Seacole House
91 Clapham High Street
London SW4 7TB
071–926 1000

Useful Contacts

Lambeth Disabled Advice Phone-in Service
071–582 4352

Lewisham

London Borough of Lewisham
Department of Social Services
Eros House
Brownhill Road
Catford, London SE6 2EG
081–695 6000

Useful Contacts

Lewisham Association of People with
  Disabilities
67 Engleheart Road
London SE6 2HN
081–698 3775 (minicom: 081–698 7384)

Merton

London Borough of Merton
Department of Personal Services
Crown House
London Road
Morden, Surrey SM4 5DX
081–543 2222

Useful Contacts

Merton Association for the Disabled
The Vestry Hall
London Road
Mitcham, Surrey CR4 3UD
081–685 1618

Newham

London Borough of Newham
Department of Social Services
99 The Grove
Stratford, London E15 1HR
081–534 4545

Useful Contacts

Newham Association for the Disabled
Durning Hall
Earlham Grove
London E7 9AB
081–519 8595

Redbridge

London Borough of Redbridge
Personal Services Directorate
17–23 Clements Road
Ilford, Essex IG1 1BL
081–478 3020

Useful Contacts

Redbridge Association for Handicapped
  People
Disability Advice Centre
Aldborough Road North
Newbury Park, Ilford IG2 7SR
081–503 8956

Richmond upon Thames

London Borough of Richmond upon
  Thames
Richmond Advice and Information for
  Disability (RAID)
Annexe Day Centre
Fortescue House
Stanley Road
Twickenham TW1 5PZ
081–898 4225

Southwark

London Borough of Southwark
Department of Social Services
49 Grange Walk
London SE1 3DY
071–525 5000

Useful Contacts

Southwark Disablement Association
2 Bradenham Close
London SE17 2QB
071–701 1391

Sutton

London Borough of Sutton
Department of Social Services
Civic Offices
St. Nicholas Way
Sutton SM1 1EA
071–770 5000

Useful Contacts

Disability Action Sutton
Sutton West Centre
Robin Hood Lane
Sutton SM1 2SD
081–643 6059

Tower Hamlets

London Borough of Tower Hamlets
Department of Social Services
Southern Grove Lodge
Southern Grove
London E3 4PN
081–980 7111

Waltham Forest

London Borough of Waltham Forest
Department of Social Services
Municipal Offices
High Road
Leyton, London E10 5QJ
081–527 5544

Useful Contacts

Waltham Forest Association for People with
   Disabilities
1A Warner Road
Walthamstow, London E17 7DY
081–509 0812 (voice & minicom)

DIAL Waltham Forest
Disability Resource Centre
1A Warner Road
London E17 7DY
081–520 4111

Wandsworth

London Borough of Wandsworth
Department of Social Services
Welbeck House
Wandsworth High Street
London SW18 2PS
081–871 6000

Useful Contacts

DIAL Wandsworth
Disabled Advice Service
Atheldene Centre
305 Garratt Lane
London SW18 4DU
081–870 7437

Westminster

Westminster City Council
Department of Social Services
Westminster City Hall
Victoria Street
London SW1E 6QP
071–828 8070

Useful Contacts

Disability Action Westminster
41 Chippenham Road
London W9 2AH
071–266 2143

DIAL Westminster
Westminster Disabled Information Service
10 Warwick Row
London SW1E 5EP
071–630 5994

▶ SCOTLAND

Major National Disability and Voluntary Organisations

Age Concern Scotland
54A Fountainbridge
Edinburgh EH3 9PT
031–228 5656

GEOGRAPHICAL DIRECTORY

British Red Cross (BRC)
Scottish Branch
14 Elliot Place
Glasgow G3 8EP
041–221 6195

Brittle Bone Society, Scotland
Ward 8
Strathmartin Hospital
Strathmartin
Dundee DD3 0PG
0382–67603

Cancerlink
9 Castle Terrace
Edinburgh EH1 2DP
031–228 5557

Chest Heart & Stroke Association
65 North Castle Street
Edinburgh EH2 3LT
031–220 6313

Citizens Advice Scotland
26 George Square
Edinburgh EH8 9LD
031–667 0156

DIAL Scotland
Braid House
Day Centre
Labrador Avenue
Howden East, Livingston
Lothian EH54 6BU
0506–33468

Disabled Income Group (DIG) Scotland
E.C.A.S. House
28–30 Howden Street
Edinburgh EH8 9HW
031–667 0249

Disability Scotland
Princes House
5 Shandwick Place
Edinburgh EH2 4RG
031–229 8632

Epilepsy Association of Scotland
National Headquarters
48 Govan Road
Glasgow G51 1JL
041–427 4911

Multiple Sclerosis Society in Scotland
2A North Charlotte Street
Edinburgh EH2 4HR
031–225 3600

Order of St. John
Priory of Scotland
St. John House
21 St. John Street
Edinburgh EH8 9DG
031–556 8711

PHAB Scotland
Princes House
5 Shandwick Place
Edinburgh EH2 4RG
031–229 3559

St. Andrews Ambulance Association
St. Andrews House
48 Milton Street
Glasgow G4 0HR
041–332 4031

Scottish Association for Mental Health
Atlantic House
38 Gardners Crescent
Edinburgh EH3 9DQ
031–229 9687

Scottish Council for Spastics
22 Corstorphine Road
Edinburgh EH1 6HP
031–337 9876

Scottish Council for Voluntary Organisations
  (SCVO)
18–19 Clarement Crescent
Edinburgh EH7 4QD
031–556 3882

Scottish National Institute for War Blinded
PO Box 500
Gillespie Crescent
Edinburgh EH10 4HZ
031–229 1456

Scottish Society for the Mentally
  Handicapped
13 Elmbank Street
Glasgow G2 4QA
041–226 4541

Scottish Spina Bifida Association
190 Queensferry Road
Edinburgh EH4 2BW
031–332 0743

Scottish Spinal Cord Injury Association
Unit 22
100 Elderpark Street
Glasgow G11 3TR
041–440 0960

Scottish Sports Association for the Disabled
Fife Institute PRE
Viewfield Road
Glenrothes, Fife KY6 2RA
0592–771700

WRVS Scottish HQ
19 Grosvenor Crescent
Edinburgh EH12 5EL
031–337 2261

SCOTTISH REGIONS

Borders

Social Work Department
Borders Regional Council
St Dunstan's
Melrose, Roxburghshire TD6 9RU
0896–82 2821

Public Transport Officer
Department of Roads & Transportation
Borders Regional Council
Regional Headquarters
Newtown St Boswells
Melrose, Roxburghshire TD6 OSA
0835–23301

Useful Contacts

Borders Disability Trust
Toll House
Maxton
Melrose, Roxburghshire TD6 ORL
0835–22231

Ettrick & Lauderdale Association of
  Voluntary Service
Voluntary Centre
6 Roxburgh Street
Galashiels TD1 1PF
0896–2787

Central

Social Work Department
Central Regional Council
Langgarth, Stirling FK8 2HA
0786–442000

Public Transport Coordination Department
Central Regional Council
Viewforth, Stirling FK8 2ET
0786–442000

Useful Contacts

Council on Disability (Stirling District)
Norman MacEwan Centre
Cameronian Street
Stirling FK8 2DX
0786–62178

DIAL Falkirk
2 Bean Row
Falkirk FK1 2PQ
0324–611567

Disability Information Service
Central Regional Council
Dundas Resource Centre
Oxgang Road
Grangemouth FK3 9EF
0786–70300

GEOGRAPHICAL DIRECTORY

Falkirk District Association for Mental
  Health
102 Thornhill Road
Falkirk FK2 7AE
0324–29955

Falkirk Voluntary Action Resource
Unit H, 54–58 Cow Wynd
Falkirk FK1 1PU
0324–365712

TAXICARD Scheme
Department of Roads & Transportation
Viewforth, Stirling FK8 2ET
0786–442000

Dumfries & Galloway

Social Work Department
Dumfries & Galloway Regional Council
8 Gordon Street
Dumfries DG1 1EG
0387–61234

Department of Roads & Transport
Dumfries & Galloway Regional Council
Council Offices
English Street
Dumfries DG1 2DD
0387–61234

Useful Contacts

Dumfries & Galloway Council on Disability
Loreburn Hall
Newall Terrace
Dumfries DG1 1LN
0387–65599

Fife

Social Work Headquarters
Fife Regional Council
North Street
Glenrothes, Fife KY7 5LT
0592–754411

Public Transport Coordination
Department of Engineering
Fife Regional Council
Fife House, North Street
Glenrothes KY7 5LT
0592–754411

Useful Contacts

Voluntary Organisations Regional Advisory
  Group (VORAG)
189 Nicol Street
Kirkaldy KY1 1PF
0592–200762

Grampian

Social Work Department
Grampian Regional Council
Woodhill House
Westburn Road
Aberdeen AB9 2LU
0224–682222

Public Transport Unit
Grampian Regional Council
Woodhill House
Westburn Road
Aberdeen AB9 2LU
0224–682222

Useful Contacts

Hillylands Disabled Living Centre
Croft Road
Mastrick, Aberdeen AB2 6RB
0224–685247

Highland

Social Work Department
Highland Regional Council
18 Hilton Village
Inverness IV2 4HT
0463–712209

Roads & Transportation Department
Highland Regional Council
Glenurquhart Road
Inverness IV3 5NX
0463–234121

Useful Contacts

Inverness Voluntary Organisations Group
David Whyte House
57 Church Street
Inverness IV1 1DR
0463–220922

Ross & Cromarty Council of Voluntary
 Service
c/o East Ross & Black Isle Council of Social
 Service
1 Castle Street
Dingwall IV15 9HU
0349–62431

Lothian

Social Work Department
Lothian Regional Council
Shrubhill House
Shrub Place, Edinburgh EH7 4PD
031–554 4301

Transport Planning Manager
Lothian Regional Council
12 St Giles Street
Edinburgh EH1 1PT
031–229 9292

Busline (in and through Lothian)
031–225 3858

Useful Contacts

DIAL Livingston
Lammermuir House
Owen Square
Almondvale EH54 6PW
0506–414472

DIAL West Lothian
2 Hopetoun Lane
Bathgate EH48 4PP
0506–635045

HANDICABS Lothian
58 Canaan Lane
Edinburgh EH10 4SG
031–447 9949

Linking Education & Disability (LEAD)
Queen Margaret College
Clerwood Terrace
Edinburgh EH12 8TS
031–339 5408

Lothian Coalition of Disabled People
13 Johnston Terrace
Edinburgh EH1 2PW
031–220 6855

Strathclyde

Social Work Department
Strathclyde Regional Council
20 India Street
Glasgow G2 4PF
041–204 2900

Public Transport Officer
Passenger Needs Section
Strathclyde PTE
Consort House
12 West George Street
Glasgow G2 1HN
041–332 6811

Useful Contacts

Centre for Independent Living
Community Services Centre
Queen Street
Paisley, Strathclyde PA1 2TU
041–887 0597

DIAL East Kilbride
96 Main Street
East Kilbride G74 4JY
0355–222955

Glasgow Association for the Welfare of the
 Disabled
c/o Red Cross HQ, 14 Elliott Place
Glasgow G3 8EP
041–221 6195

Glasgow Forum on Disability
McIver House
51 Cadogan Street
Glasgow G2 7QB
041–227 6125

Information & Resource Centre
90 High Blantyre Road
Burnbank, Hamilton ML3 9HW
0698–825546

Mid Lanarkshire Access Group for the
  Disabled
51 Margaretvale Drive
Larkhall, Lanarkshire ML9 1QH
0698–881201

Strathclyde Transport Travel Centre
St Enoch Square
Central Glasgow G1
041–226 4826

Strathkelvin Contact Point
Woodhead Community Education Centre
Woodhead Park
Kirkintilloch G66 3DD
041–776 0068

Tayside

Social Work Department
Tayside Regional Council
Tayside House
28 Crichton Street
Dundee DD1 3RN
0382–23281

Useful Contacts

Transport Unit
Roads & Transport Department
Parker Street
Dundee DD1 5RW
0382–303006

Disabled & Carers Association (Dundee)
Telephone House
21 Ward Road
Dundee DD1 1ND
0345–090113

Dundee Voluntary Action
Castle Hill House
1 High Street
Dundee DD1 lTD
0382–21545

Perth Council for the Disabled
Inverearn
Abernethie PH2 9JZ
073885–261

Perth & Kinross Access Group
(DIAL Perth)
Letham Clinic
Marles Road
Perth PH1 2HL
0738–39134

Island Councils

Social Work Department (HQ)
Orkney Islands Council
Council Offices
Kirkwall, Orkney KW15 1NY
0856–873535

Social Work Department
Shetland Islands Council
92 St Olaf Street
Lerwick, Shetland ZE1 OEN
0595–3535

Social Work Department
Western Isles Island Council
Sandwick Road
Stornoway
Isle of Lewis PA87 2BW
0851–703773

Useful Contacts

Council on Disability for Shetland
Harbour House
Esplanade
Lerwick, Shetland ZE1 OLL
0595–2196

Lewis & Harris Council on Disability
c/o Lewis Council of Social Services
71–77 Cromwell Street
Stornoway PA87 2BW
0851–702632

Skye & Lochalsh Association for Disability
North Skye Centre
c/o Red Cross Centre
Staffin Road
Portree, Isle of Skye
0478–2676

WALES

Major National Disability and Voluntary Organisations

British Red Cross Society
National Headquarters
9 Grosvenor Crescent
London SW1X 7EJ
071–235 5454

St. John Ambulance Brigade
Priory for Wales
Priory House
Lisvane Road
Llanishen, Cardiff CF1 7JW
0222–750222

PHAB Wales
First Floor
178 Penarth Road
Cardiff CF1 7JW
0222–223677

SEQUAL
Ddol Heir
Glyn Ceiriog
Llangollen, Clwyd LL20 7NP
0691–72331

Wales Council for the Blind
Shand House
22 Newport Road
Cardiff CF2 1YB
0222–473954

Wales Council for the Deaf
Maritime Offices
Woodland Terrace
Maesycoed
Pontypridd, Mid Glamorgan CF37 1DZ
0443–485687

Wales Council for the Disabled
Llys Ifor
Crescent Road
Caerphilly, Mid Glamorgan CF8 3SL
0222–887325/6/7

Wales Mind CYMRA
National Association for Mental Health
23 St. Mary Street
Cardiff CF1 2AA
0222–395123

Womens Royal Voluntary Service (WRVS)
Welsh Headquarters
26 Cathedral Road
Cardiff CF1 9LJ
0222–228386

WELSH COUNTIES

Clwyd

Department of Social Services
Clwyd County Council
Shire Hall
Mold, Clwyd CH7 6NB
0352–752121

Transportation Officer
Highways & Transportation Department
Clwyd County Council
Shire Hall
Mold, Clwyd CH7 6NF
0352–752121

Useful Contacts

Clwyd Association for the Disabled
Clwyd Voluntary Services Council
Station Road
Ruthin, Clwyd LL15 1BP
08242–2441 or 08242–3805

Dyfed

Department of Social Services
Dyfed County Council
3 Red Street
Camarthen SA31 1QL
0267–233333

Assistant County Surveyor, Transportation
Highways & Transportation Department
Dyfed County Council
Camarthen, Dyfed SA31 3LZ
0267–233333 ext.4335

Useful Contacts

Dyfed Association for the Disabled
'Morlais'
Llechryd
Cardigan, Dyfed SA43 2NJ
0239–87343

Gwent

Department of Social Services
Gwent County Council
County Hall
Cwmbran, Gwent NP44 2XE
0633–838838

Section Head, Transportation
County Planning Department
Gwent County Council
County Hall
Cwmbran, Gwent NP44 2XF
0633–832478

Useful Contacts

Blaenau Gwent Council for the Disabled
22 Mount Pleasant Road
Ebbw Vale, Gwent NP3 6JH
0495–309036

Gwynedd

Department of Social Services
Gwynedd County Council
Shire Hall Street
Caernarfon LL55 1SH
0286–672255

Public Transport Coordinator
County Planning Department
Gwynedd County Council
County Offices
Shire Hall Street
Caernarfon LL55 1SH
0286–679378

Useful Contacts

Gwynedd Association for the Disabled
Gwynedd Voluntary Services
Bryn Morsa, South Road
Caernarfon LL55 2YH
0286–2626

Mid Glamorgan

Department of Social Services
Mid Glamorgan County Council
County Council Offices
Greyfriars Road
Cardiff CF1 3LL
0222–820820

Assistant County Transport Officer
Joint Transportation Unit
Mid Glamorgan County Council
County Council Offices
Greyfriars Road
Cardiff CF1 3LL
0222–820820

Useful Contacts

DIAL Llantrisant
Cowbridge Road
Talbot Green
Pont-y-clun, Mid Glamorgan CF7 8HL
0443–237937

DIAL Merthyr Tydfil
Ty-Gwyn Day Centre
Church Street
Merthyr Tydfil, Mid Glamorgan CF47 OEE
0685–79769

Powys

Department of Social Services
Powys County Council
County Hall
Llandrindod Wells, Powys LD1 5LG
0597–826000

Highways & Transportation Department
Powys County Council
County Hall
Llandrindod Wells, Powys LD1 5LG
0597–826000

Useful Contacts

Brecknock Association for Disabled People
c/o Powys Rural Council
Watton Mount
Brecon, Powys LD3 7AW
0874–622631

South Glamorgan

Department of Social Services
South Glamorgan County Council
County Hall
Atlantic Wharf
Cardiff CF1 5UW
0222–872000

Group Leader, Public Transport
Environment and Planning Department
South Glamorgan County Council
County Hall
Atlantic Wharf
Cardiff CF1 5UW
0222–873250

Useful Contacts

Disabled Living Centre
The Lodge, Rookwood Hospital
Llandaff, Cardiff CF5 2YN
0222–566281 ext.3751

West Glamorgan

Department of Social Services
West Glamorgan County Council
County Hall
Oystermouth Road
Swansea SA1 3SN
0792–471111

Senior Assistant Director, Transportation
   Services
Environment & Highways Department
West Glamorgan County Council
County Hall
Oystermouth Road
Swansea SA1 3SN
0792–471111

Useful Contacts

DIAL Swansea
Brondeg House
St Johns Road
Mansetton, Swansea SA5 8PR
0792–587642

APPENDIX B

▶ **USEFUL PUBLICATIONS**

8 MPH VEHICLES – YOUR RIGHTS AND RESPONSIBILITIES
Available from the DoT Disability Unit (Tel. 071–276 5257)

AA GUIDE FOR THE DISABLED TRAVELLER
Available from the AA (Tel. 0345–500600)

ACCESS AROUND LONDON FOR DISABLED PEOPLE
Leaflet free of charge from London Transport's (LT's) Unit for Disabled Passengers (071–222 5600)

ACCESS AT THE CHANNEL PORTS – A GUIDE FOR DISABLED PEOPLE
Available from RADAR (Tel. 071–637 5400)

ACCESS BUS – TRANSPORT FOR THE COMMUNITY: a guide to community bus services in Surrey.
Available free of charge from Surrey County Council (Tel. 081–541 9482)

ACCESS IN LONDON
Published by Nicolson and available from bookshops

ACCESS TO THE DOCKLANDS LIGHT RAILWAY
A cassette tape available from LT's Unit for Disabled Passengers (Tel. 071–222 5600)

ACCESS TO THE UNDERGROUND
Available by post from the Unit for Disabled Passengers at London Transport (Tel. 071–222 5600)

AIRPORT/HOTEL TRANSFER
Available from LT's Unit for Disabled Passengers (Tel. 071–222 5600)

ALTERNATIVE TRANSPORT SCHEMES – a guide to transport schemes in Buckinghamshire.
Available from Bucks Council for Voluntary Service (Tel. 0296–21036) or Bucks County Council (Tel. 0296–382000)

AROUND LANCASHIRE BY RAIL
Available free of charge from Lancashire County Council (Tel. 0772–264582/3)

BRITISH RAIL AND DISABLED TRAVELLERS
Available from stations and Travel Centres

CARE IN THE AIR – ADVICE FOR HANDICAPPED TRAVELLERS
Available free of charge from the ATUC (Tel. 071–242 3882)

CARELINK
Available free of charge from LT's Unit for Disabled Passengers (Tel. 071–222 5600)

CHOOSING AN ELECTRIC WHEELCHAIR – NOTES FOR PRIVATE BUYERS
Available for DLF (Tel. 071–289 6111)

COMMUNITY TRANSPORT REGISTER: a guide to transport in Surrey.
Available free of charge from the Surrey Voluntary Service Council (Tel. 0483–66072)

DIRECTORY FOR DISABLED PEOPLE
Available from RADAR (Tel. 071–637 5400) and bookshops

USEFUL PUBLICATIONS

DIRECTORY OF GROUPS AND ORGANISATIONS WITH TRANSPORT FOR ELDERLY AND DISABLED PEOPLE IN LEICESTERSHIRE
Available free of charge from DIAL Leicester, 76 Clarendon Park Road, Leicester, LE2 3AD.

DIRECTORY OF RURAL TRANSPORT SCHEMES: a guide to transport schemes in Oxfordshire.
Available free of charge from the Transport Officer at Oxfordshire Rural Community Council (Tel. 0865–512488)

DIRECTORY OF TRANSPORT IN SCOTLAND
Available free of charge from Disability Scotland (Tel. 031–229 8632)

DIRECTORY OF VOLUNTARY AND COMMUNITY TRANSPORT
Available free of charge from the Disability Unit at the Department of Transport (Tel. 071–276 5257)

DIRECTORY OF VOLUNTARY TRANSPORT PROVISION IN CUMBRIA
Available free of charge from Cumbria Transport Forum Tel. 0539–729168)

DIRECTORY OF WILTSHIRE COMMUNITY TRANSPORT SCHEMES AND OF TRANSPORT FACILITIES FOR THE ELDERLY AND DISABLED
Available free of charge from the Dept of Planning and Highways at County Hall (Tel. 0225–753641 Ext. 3454)

DISABILITY RIGHTS HANDBOOK
Available from the Disability Alliance (Tel. 071–247 8776)

DISABLED PERSON'S RAILCARD
Leaflet available from BR stations, Travel Centres and main Post Offices

DISCOUNTS AND CONCESSIONS FACT SHEET NO. 9
Available from RADAR (Tel. 071–637 5400)

DURHAM – a guide to transport services in Durham to be published in 1992, enquiries to Durham Public Transport and Environment Dept., tel. 091–386 4411 Ext. 2212

EQUIPMENT AND SERVICES FOR PEOPLE WITH DISABILITIES: DH LEAFLET HB6
Available free of charge from Departments of Social Security offices (SHHD in Scotland).

EQUIPMENT FOR DISABLED PEOPLE, WHEELCHAIRS
Available from the Disability Information Trust (Tel. 0865–750103)

FACTSHEET NO 2: on motor tax exemption
Available from RADAR (Tel. 071–637 5400)

FACTSHEET NO 3: on motor tax relief
Available from RADAR (Tel. 071–637 5400)

FACTSHEET NO 6: Advice on motor insurance for disabled drivers
Available from RADAR (Tel. 071–637 5400)

FLIGHT PLAN – HINTS FOR AIRLINE PASSENGERS
Available free of charge from the ATUC (Tel. 071–242 3882)

GETTING ABOUT IN HAMPSHIRE
Available from the Passenger Transport Group of Hampshire County Council (Tel. 0962–846983)

GETTING AROUND – a guide for people with a mobility problem in the West Midlands (also on cassette)
Available free of charge from Centro (Tel. 021–200 2700 – Birmingham or 0203–559559 – Coventry)

GETTING THERE – A GUIDE TO PUBLIC TRANSPORT FOR PEOPLE WITH A MOBILITY PROBLEM
Available free of charge from Cheshire County Council (Tel. 0244–603742)

GOING PLACES – A GUIDE TO TRANSPORT FACILITIES FOR DISABLED PEOPLE IN DERBYSHIRE
Available free of charge from Derbyshire County Council (Tel. 0629–580000 Ext. 6741)

GUIDE FOR THE WAR DISABLED: DSS LEAFLET MPL 153
Available free of charge from Departments of Social Security offices

GUIDE TO BRITISH RAIL FOR DISABLED PEOPLE
Available from RADAR (Tel. 071–637 5400)

GUIDE TO HEATHROW AIRPORT FOR PEOPLE WITH SPECIAL NEEDS
Available free of charge from Heathrow Travel Care (Tel. 081–745 7495)

GUIDE TO SERVICES IN THE UK OFFERING ADVICE, INFORMATION AND ASSESSMENT TO DISABLED AND ELDERLY MOTORISTS
Available from MAVIS (Tel. 0344–770456 OR 770463)

GUIDE TO TRANSPORT SERVICES IN DEVON
Available free of charge from Devon County Council (Tel. 0392–382123)

GUIDE TO WELFARE TRANSPORT IN ESSEX
Available free of charge from the Planning Dept of Essex County Council (Tel. 0245–492211)

HAPPY TO HELP
Guide available from The Corporate Affairs Dept., Dover Harbour Board, Cambridge Terrace, Dover, Kent, CT17 9BJ. (Tel. 0304–240400 Ext. 4807)

HEALTH ADVICE FOR TRAVELLERS IN THE EUROPEAN COMMUNITY (T2)
Available from the Dept of Health (Tel. 0800–555777)

HEALTH ADVICE FOR TRAVELLERS OUTSIDE THE EUROPEAN COMMUNITY (T3)
Available from the Dept of Health (Tel. 0800–555777)

HELP WITH MOBILITY: GETTING AROUND: DSS LEAFLET HB4
Available free of charge from Departments of Social Security offices (SHHD in Scotland).

HELPING PEOPLE WHO ARE DEAF AS WELL AS BLIND
Available from the RNIB (Tel. 071–388 1266)

HERTFORDSHIRE – a guide to transport to be published during 1992.
Enquiries to Passenger Transport Unit (Tel. 0992–588172)

HOW TO CHOOSE A PAVEMENT VEHICLE
Available from the Banstead Mobility Centre (Tel. 081–770 1151)

HOW TO GUIDE A BLIND PERSON
Available from the RNIB (Tel. 071–388 1266)

HOW TO PUSH A WHEELCHAIR
Available from the West Midlands Disabled Motorists Club (Tel. 0743–761889)

HOW TO TALK TO A DEAF-BLIND PERSON
Available from the National Deaf-Blind League (Tel. 0733 573511)

LEAFLET V188: on motor tax exemption
Available from DVLC (Tel. 0792–772134)

LINCOLNSHIRE: a guide to transport to be published during 1992.
Enquiries to County Transport Agency at Lincolnshire County Council (Tel. 0522–553132)

LONDON FOR ALL – INFORMATION FOR PEOPLE WITH DISABILITIES
available free of charge from the London Tourist Board and Convention Centre (Tel. 071–730 3488)

MANUAL WHEELCHAIRS: LIST 14
Available from Disability Scotland (Tel. 031–229 8632)

MOBILITY GUIDE FOR BUCKINGHAMSHIRE
Available free from the Bucks Council for Voluntary Service. (Tel. 0296–21036)

MOTORAIL
Leaflet available at principal stations, Travel Centres and travel agents

MOTORING AND MOBILITY FOR DISABLED PEOPLE
Available from RADAR (Tel. 071–637 5400) or ask your local DLC

NHS HOSPITAL TRAVEL COSTS: DSS LEAFLET H11
Available free of charge from Departments of Social Security offices

ON THE MOVE – a guide to mobility in Northern Ireland
Available from Disability Action. (Tel. 0232–491011)

ORANGE BADGE SCHEME – RECIPROCAL PARKING ARRANGEMENTS FOR DISABLED AND BLIND PEOPLE IN EUROPE
Available free of charge from the Department of Transport (Tel. 071–276 6291)

PEOPLE IN WHEELCHAIRS – HINTS FOR HELPERS
Available from the BRCS (Tel. 071–235 5454)

PERSONAL TOILET ON LONG FLIGHTS
Available from the DLF (Tel. 071–289 6111)

PLANE EASY
A tape and leaflet available from the RNIB (Tel. 071–388 1266). Also available in braille.

POWERED WHEELCHAIRS: LIST 15
Available from Disability Scotland (Tel. 031–229 8632)

SICK OR DISABLED? DSS LEAFLET HB5
Available free of charge from Departments of Social Security offices (SHHD in Scotland).

SICK OR INJURED THROUGH SERVICE IN THE ARMED FORCES: DSS LEAFLET FB16
Available free of charge from Departments of Social Security offices (SHHD in Scotland).

SOCIAL SECURITY: DSS LEAFLET HB5
Available free of charge from Departments of Social Security offices (SHHD in Scotland), this leaflet is a guide to non-contributory benefits for disabled people

SURVIVAL GUIDE FOR PEOPLE WITH PHYSICAL DISABILTIES
Published by Dominique Joyeux. (Tel. 0234–271087)

TAYSIDE – guide to transport to be published during 1992.
Enquiries to the Transport Unit of Tayside Regional Council (Tel. 0382–303006)

TRANSPORT DIRECTORY FOR THE MOBILITY IMPAIRED: a guide to transport in Kent.
Available free of charge from Kent County Council (Tel. 0622–671411)

TRANSPORT IN LOTHIAN
Available free of charge from Lothian Regional Council (Tel. 031–225 3858)

TRANSPORT INFORMATION AND REGULATIONS – transport information for Scotland.
Available free of charge from Disability Scotland (Tel. 031–229 8632)

TRAVEL GUIDE: a guide to transport for elderly and disabled people in Gloucestershire.
Available free of charge from the Public Transport Manager of Gloucs County Council (Tel. 0452–452609)

VAT 701/7/86 and NOTICE 670
Leaflets available from HM Customs and Excise

WALKING AIDS LIST 9
Available free of charge from the DLF (Tel. 071–289 6111)

WALKING EQUIPMENT LIST 13
Availble from Disability Scotland (Tel. 031–229 8632)

WHAT YOU NEED TO KNOW ABOUT DRIVER LICENCING
Available from your local post office or the Driver Enquiry Unit, DVLC, Swansea, SA6 7JL (Tel. 0792–772151)

WHEELCHAIRS AND THEIR USE – A GUIDE TO CHOOSING A WHEELCHAIR
Available from RADAR (Tel. 071–637 5400)

WHEELCHAIRS: LIST 10
Available free of charge from the DLF (Tel. 071–289 6111)

WHICH BENEFIT? DSS LEAFLET FB2
Available from Departments of Social Security offices (SHHD in Scotland).

▶ PUBLISHERS' ADDRESSES

Age Concern England
1268 London Road
Norbury
London SW16 4ER

Automobile Association
Fanum House
Basingstoke, Hants. RG21 2EA

Bus & Coach Council
Sardinia House
Bus & Coach Council
Sardinia House
52 Lincoln's Inn Fields
London WC2A 3LZ

Department of Transport (DoT)
  Disability Unit
Room S10/21, 2 Marsham Street
London SW1P 3EB

Disability Alliance (ERA)
Universal House
89–94 Wentworth Street
London E1 7SA

Robert Nicholson PLC
77–85 Fulham Palace Road
London W6 8JB

Royal Association for Disability &
  Rehabilitation (RADAR)
25 Mortimer Street
London W1N 8AB

Royal Automobile Club (RAC)
PO Box 700, Spectrum
Pond Street
Bristol, Avon BS99 1RB

Spinal Injuries Association
Newpoint House
76 St James Lane
London N10 3DF

TRIPSCOPE
63 Esmond Road
London W4 1JE
and
Pamwell House
160 Pennywell Road
Bristol BS5 0TX

APPENDIX C – SUBJECT INDEX

SUBJECT INDEX

SUBJECT INDEX

Printed in the United Kingdom for HMSO
Dd294553 C200 11/92 39462 56-5813